DOES FRANCE STILL COUNT?

THE WASHINGTON PAPERS

... intended to meet the need for an authoritative, yet prompt, public appraisal of the major developments in world affairs.

President, CSIS: David M. Abshire

Series Editor: Walter Laqueur

Director of Studies: Erik R. Peterson

Director of Publications: Nancy B. Eddy

Managing Editor: Donna R. Spitler

MANUSCRIPT SUBMISSION

The Washington Papers and Praeger Publishers welcome inquiries concerning manuscript submissions. Please include with your inquiry a curriculum vitae, synopsis, table of contents, and estimated manuscript length. Manuscript length must fall between 120 and 200 double-spaced typed pages. All submissions will be peer reviewed. Submissions to *The Washington Papers* should be sent to *The Washington Papers*; The Center for Strategic and International Studies; 1800 K Street NW; Suite 400; Washington, DC 20006. Book proposals should be sent to Praeger Publishers; 90 Post Road West; P.O. Box 5007; Westport, CT 06881-5007.

The Washington Papers/164

DOES FRANCE STILL COUNT?

The French Role in the New Europe

Steven Philip Kramer

Foreword by
Samuel F. Wells Jr.

PUBLISHED WITH
THE CENTER FOR STRATEGIC
AND INTERNATIONAL STUDIES
WASHINGTON, D.C.

PRAEGER

Westport, Connecticut
London

Library of Congress Cataloging-in-Publication Data

Kramer, Steven Philip.
    Does France still count? : the French role in the New Europe /
Steven Philip Kramer.
        p.   cm. — (Washington papers ; 164)
    Includes index.
    ISBN 0-275-95060-3. — ISBN 0-275-95061-1 (pbk.)
    1. France—Foreign relations—1981-   2. Europe—Foreign
relations—1989-   3. International cooperation.   4. Self
-determination, National—France.   5. France—Foreign relations—
Germany.   6. Germany—Foreign relations—France.   7. World
politics—1989-   I. Title.   II. Series.
DC423.K73   1994
327.44—dc20   94-22127

British Library Cataloging-in-Publication data is available.

Library of Congress Catalog Card Number: 94-22127
ISBN: 0-275-95060-3 (cloth)
        0-275-95061-1 (paper)

First published in 1994

Praeger Publishers, 88 Post Road West, Westport, CT 06881
An imprint of Greenwood Publishing Group, Inc.

Printed in the United States of America

The paper used in this book complies with the Permanent
Paper Standard issued by the National Information Standards
Organization (Z39.48-1984).

10   9   8   7   6   5   4   3   2   1

To Maria

Contents

Foreword

To most Americans who think about the issue, France has long appeared difficult and unpredictable in its international behavior. It lost three wars to Germany, yet after 1945 French leaders resisted U.S. leadership of the West, and in 1966 General Charles de Gaulle withdrew France from NATO's integrated military command. In major crises over Berlin and Cuba, Paris accepted Washington's leadership and stood with its allies. But in many other areas, France went its own way and was often critical of U.S. policy. Many American leaders resented France for getting a free ride within a Western security regime in which the United States assumed much of the responsibility for leadership and initiative, took most of the risks, and paid a disproportionate share of the costs.

With the end of the cold war, the premises of French international policy collapsed. France no longer had room to maneuver between the contending superpowers. German unification made France's neighbor the most powerful country in Europe, and it appeared that the remaining superpower might play a greatly reduced role in Europe. France adjusted quickly to the new circumstances and worked to deepen European integration through the Maastricht Treaty. But resistance in Europe and in France itself as well as applications to widen membership of the European Community (now Union) challenged the French strategy.

In this incisive book, Steven Philip Kramer shows why the French shaped their policy as they did during the cold war and how they have reshaped it since 1989. He shows clearly the central importance of the Franco-German partnership and argues persuasively that this cooperation is vital for the success of European integration and worthy of strong U.S. support. He explains how French leaders decided "to trade sovereignty for influence" in subordinating national policy to European integration.

American leaders and concerned citizens can learn a great deal from this brief volume. Kramer shows that France does still count and that it is the only other power in the world today able and willing to play a global role. French actions in Cambodia, Bosnia, Somalia, and Rwanda demonstrate a commitment to international activism. The United States would do well to develop cooperation with Paris as a way of lessening its own burden in world affairs while maintaining its influence in Europe.

Samuel F. Wells Jr.
Woodrow Wilson Center
Washington, D.C.

About the Author

Steven Philip Kramer is professor of history at the Industrial College of the Armed Forces, National Defense University, Washington, D.C., where he offers courses in modern history and European affairs. He also teaches at Georgetown University and the Johns Hopkins School of Advanced International Studies.

Dr. Kramer taught European history at the University of New Mexico from 1975 to 1988. He served as a Council of Foreign Relations fellow in the U.S. Department of State (1983–1984), directed the Face to Face program of the Carnegie Endowment for International Peace (1986–1987), and was a fellow at Woodrow Wilson Center (1989). Most recently, he was John J. McCloy Distinguished Fellow in Residence at the American Institute for Contemporary German Studies (1990–1991) and fellow at the Institute for the Study of Diplomacy at Georgetown University (1992). Dr. Kramer has written widely on European politics and culture, including a book on European socialism and another on the French filmmaker Abel Gance. He received his Ph.D. in history from Princeton University in 1971.

Acknowledgments

I thank Julius Friend, Josef Konvitz, Irene Kyriakopoulos, Bowman Miller, Kim Pendleton, and Sam Wells for their valuable critiques of the draft manuscript. I am also indebted to the many friends and colleagues who have shared their interest in France and Europe with me, as well as French and European governmental and nongovernmental officials who have provided so much insight. Eric Lebédel of the Quai d'Orsay deserves special mention. Portions of earlier versions of this manuscript have appeared in *The Washington Quarterly* and *The World Today*; an earlier version of chapter 3 was prepared for the Institute for National Strategic Studies, and an earlier version of chapter 5 was circulated privately by the Jean Monnet Council.

I thank the administration and faculty of the Industrial College of the Armed Forces for providing a climate that encourages research and writing.

Translations from the French are my own.

Summary

France's political leaders have been deeply committed
to both maintaining France's independence and asserting
its leadership role in Europe. The end of the cold war
and the demise of the "Europe of Yalta"—so often criticized
by France—as well as the unification of Germany forced
France to rethink its European and international strate-
gies. The major theme of this book is France's effort to
redefine its role in the post-cold war era—above all by
deepening European integration—and what that means to
France, to Europe, and to the United States. The book
examines France's international role after the cold war to
answer the question raised by its title—does France still
count?

The end of the cold war and the unification of Germany
took France by surprise. Despite complaints about the "Europe of Yalta," the French had made the most of the postwar situation. Germany, France's "hereditary enemy," had
become its closest partner. The Franco-German couple
had become the basis for a West European community that

The views expressed in this book are those of the author and
do not reflect the official policy of the National Defense University, the U.S. Department of Defense, or the U.S. government.

1

had moved toward complete economic integration through
the Single European Act. Although Germany was the
stronger economic power, France had become the second
largest economy in Western Europe and, through the use
of the German model of financial discipline, had almost
eliminated historic patterns of inflation. Their relationship
was complementary — Paris exerted political leadership
and Bonn economic leadership. Together, they were usually
able to get their way within the European Community
(EC).

With respect to European security, France had the
best of both worlds during the cold war. Despite former
French president Charles de Gaulle's break with the integrated military command of the North Atlantic Treaty Organization (NATO), France resumed close security relations
with both United States and NATO and could count on the
U.S. nuclear umbrella. Thanks to its independent nuclear
force, France also retained a significant degree of independence that could be parlayed into claims of European leadership and great power status. The end of the cold war and
German unification called into question this entire arrange-
ment as well as briefly evoking demons of the German
past. This volume's first two chapters examine France's
response to the new situation. Chapter 1 argues that the
long-standing desire to "moor" Germany to Europe, intensified by German unification, was the major impulse behind
France's decision to advocate deepening European integration. It describes the vision of Europe that France developed and how France and Germany cooperated in embodying a large part of this vision in the final document
adopted at Maastricht. The Treaty of Maastricht was
above all a political document, designed to anchor Germany to Europe, but the key means of doing so was monetary union.

Chapter 2 examines how France rethought its attitudes toward security in light of the cold war's end, German unification, and the Gulf War. It begins by analyzing
how before 1989 France had sought to balance its conflict-

ing desires for national independence, Atlantic cooperation, and European solidarity. It then examines how
France attempted to give a security, and eventually defense, dimension to the new European Union by reviv-
ing the Western European Union (WEU). Fearing that the
United States might withdraw from Europe, France
wanted to guarantee the existence of a multilateral European security identity to ensure that Germany would not
be tempted to develop an independent defense policy. But
French efforts to create a European Security and Defense
Identity (ESDI) led to tensions with the United States,
which feared that France was trying to push the United
States out of Europe.

The Treaty of Maastricht represented a significant victory for French diplomacy in trying to create a stable West
European order that would minimize the risks coming from
German unification. But barely was the treaty signed when
it began to run into difficulties. Chapter 3 describes the
vicissitudes experienced by France and Europe in 1992 and
1993. Ratification turned out to be a greater problem than
imagined. The Danish referendum of June 2, 1992, catalyzed fears all over Europe concerning the implications of
the treaty. Only by minimizing the treaty's intent was it
possible to ensure ratification, with the result that the
prospects for deepening European integration were both
delayed and undermined.

French president François Mitterrand tried to demonstrate French support for Maastricht through a referendum on September 20, 1992. His effort backfired, creating
a political crisis within France and a monetary crisis in
the European Monetary System (EMS). At the same time,
Europe's inability to control the warring successor states
of former Yugoslavia weakened faith in the viability of
ESDI. As if this were not enough, a second monetary crisis
in August 1993 sparked increasing tensions between
France and Germany over the Bundesbank's high interest
rates. It also raised questions about Franco-German solidarity: Did the rhetoric of Franco-German cooperation still

reflect what policymakers are thinking in private? Could France continue to tie its lackluster economy to a Bundesbank determined to maintain high interest rates? How could France hope to base a European security identity on a Eurocorps – a mixed force of primarily French and German units – when Germany was still unwilling to commit forces out of area? What kind of Europe was likely to emerge during the 1990s?

Chapter 4 raises another fundamental question. Do France's political institutions and the nature of French political life contribute to or undermine France's capacity to play the kind of grand role its leaders desire? This question is inescapable given the narrow victory of the referendum on the Treaty of Maastricht. To determine whether that first impression is borne out, chapter 4 briefly examines the role of the political institutions of the Fifth Republic that seem well suited to the conduct of foreign policy. It then analyzes the political system itself and the problems it must confront.

In the last decade, the consensus of the French political class has gone beyond foreign policy and defense to economic policy. The differences between the parties of the Left and Right, on which the political system is based, seem increasingly irrelevant. During the same period, the most serious domestic issue has been chronic high unemployment recently exacerbated by the recession. Governments of both Left and Right have pursued the same kinds of economic policies with equal lack of success, thus contributing to the sense that the state is no longer capable of defending French interests, thereby engendering a chronic sense of malaise. During the campaign on the Maastricht referendum, some politicians tried to tie France's abandonment of significant areas of national sovereignty to the state's inability to resolve its economic problems. The near success of the anti-Maastricht campaign, which marked the first direct confrontation between two new political coalitions – a party of movement and a party of reaction – opens up the prospect that the consensus of the political class could break down in a way that would threaten the continuity of France's European policy and prejudice France's international role.

Finally, chapter 5 analyzes current Franco-U.S. relations and the prospects for the future. It addresses the endemic tensions between France and the United States over the shape of the new Europe and the Atlantic partnership. It argues that the NATO Summit has laid the basis for a new security relationship between the two. Only France can lead Europe in the direction of becoming a global security partner with the United States, as opposed to a global economic superpower with merely regional security interests.

This volume concludes that, despite problems, France possesses political institutions and a political class well suited to playing a global role. But France's capacity to play this role requires a continuing Franco-German partnership as well as cooperation between Europe and the United States.

1

A French Vision of Europe: Political and Economic Integration

The end of the cold war and the unification of Germany transformed the universe in which French foreign policy operates. Although both events had been explicit French goals since the presidency of Charles de Gaulle, France did not have to confront their implications as long as the likelihood of their realization remained remote. The sudden and inexorable march to German unity and the limited French role in the process induced a brief panic among the French political elite, followed by deep pessimism. What France feared was not the resurgence of Prussianism or Nazism in Germany, but France's own marginalization. The German Question became an identity crisis for the French political class — a French Question. What was France's role to be in the New Europe? Did France still count?

France's postwar foreign policy goal has always been to maintain political leadership in Europe, both for its own sake and for the sake of whatever larger role France could play in world affairs. The new international situation soon prompted serious thinking about the French role in Europe and the world. This chapter examines the historical background of the Franco-German relationship — the focus of France's European policy since shortly after World War II. It reconstructs the mind-set that informed French policy-making in the period immediately after cold war ended and German unification occurred, the better to understand the nature of the program for European union advocated by France and developed in cooperation with Germany – a program that became the basis for the Maastricht Treaty.

The Franco-German Relationship

The key to France's European policy since 1950 has been the Franco-German relationship.[1] The creation of "Europe" starting with the Schuman Plan was the instrument of Franco-German reconciliation. And since then, the European Community has developed and prospered only when France and Germany have been able to harmonize their goals and act as the locomotive of European integration. Although French political leaders have differed and continue to differ about the kind of Europe they want to create (the two historic poles being European integration leader Jean Monnet's vision of a federal Europe and de Gaulle's conception of a Europe of States), there has been no disagreement in France about the primacy of the relationship with the Federal Republic.

That does not mean that there has been no competition; of course, the French sought to be the dominant partner. After World War II, the French economy grew and modernized rapidly compared with both its own historical performance and Europe as a whole, but surpass the Federal Republic economically it did not.[2] What France achieved was a relationship of complementarity in which Germany was the dominant economic partner, France the dominant political partner – what French political scientist Dominique Moisi has called "the balance of the bomb and the mark."[3]

France took advantage of its noneconomic assets. It had an independent nuclear force and the status of a victor of World War II, with rights in Germany and Berlin and a permanent seat in the United Nations (UN) Security Coun-

cil. After 1958, it escaped from the political instability that
had plagued it since the 1930s. The French president was
endowed with monarchical powers in foreign policy and
defense. The European Community, like the Coal and Steel
Community before it, had been largely shaped by the
French who held strong leadership roles within each. Germany still felt a need to be "legitimized" by France.

In recent years, the French implicitly accepted German economic leadership in Europe, adopting German economic and monetary policies; in this domain at least Paris
needed to be legitimized by Bonn. In return, France expected German support, or at least forbearance, on questions of "grande politique." This became easier as French
leaders ceased trying to force Germany to choose between
Atlanticism and Franco-German cooperation, a change begun under Valéry Giscard d'Estaing and completed under
François Mitterrand (although this was not always the way
Washington saw it). Under this socialist president, France
became in many ways profoundly pessimistic in its assessment of the Soviet threat and gave less ambiguous support
for the U.S. presence in Europe.[4]

Indeed, what France feared most during the 1980s was
not German predominance but Soviet expansionism and
the prospect that Germany, anxious to maintain its pre-
cious ties to the German Democratic Republic (GDR) and
Eastern Europe, would go too far in accommodating Moscow. Concern over German drift from NATO and Western
Europe motivated Mitterrand's 1983 Bundestag speech
supporting Intermediate-Range Nuclear Force (INF) deployment in Germany. Thus, the French strategy was to
anchor Germany all the more firmly to France and Europe
by closer military and economic cooperation. Examples of
the priority accorded such cooperation were the implemen-
tation of the security provisions of the Elysée Treaty of
1963 and French support for the Single European Act.

Ironically, the French were so content with their success in mooring Germany that they did not always grasp
that they were pushing through open doors. Helmut Kohl's

government did not need to have European cooperation forced upon it; unlike the French it did not suffer from the Gaullist heritage. France perceived Germany as a mirror image of itself. It was France that left the integrated NATO military command and followed an independent foreign and security policy, yet nothing worried the French more than that Germany might do the same. France played off being both autonomous and European; it may have feared that Germany would do likewise. In short, French fears of German nationalism and domination may have reflected France's difficulty in transcending its own nationalism far more than an objective threat from Germany.

The GDR's quick, unexpected end and the rapid unification of Germany caught the French, like everyone else, by surprise. France's limited role in the 2 + 4 meetings and the resolution of Germany's NATO status bilaterally between Kohl and Soviet premier Mikhail Gorbachev were hardly gratifying to the French. In such an atmosphere it is not surprising that misunderstandings were rife between the French and Germans. The experience brought out all of Mitterrand's ambivalent feelings about Germany—as well as his petulance.

In contrast to elite opinion, French public opinion strongly supported unification, even while believing that it marked the end of Franco-German "complementarity." A SOFRES poll of September 26, 1990, showed that 79 percent of the French and 82 percent of the Germans believed that a unified Germany would be stronger economically than France; 42 percent of the French and 49 percent of the Germans thought that Germany would be stronger politically (against 30 percent and 23 percent who picked France). In addition, 62 percent of the French (38 percent of the Germans) opined that a unified Germany would dominate the EC. Significantly, 57 percent of those French who were satisfied with unification believed it probable that Germany would dominate the EC![5]

It seems obvious that neither Mitterrand nor the political class would be content with a second-place role for

France. But France's hand did not appear strong in the days following unification. There was talk about a *repli national*. Fears of a dominant Germany finally forced France to transcend its most serious conflict — wanting to maintain national independence versus promoting a strong and independent Europe. The Mitterrand administration began to translate to the European level the concept of nation that France had pursued on a purely national level. The way to maximize the French role in a new Europe would be to shape its structures before the French position was eroded. And the current political situation was propitious. The foundations for such a policy were already present — the Single European Act was in the process of being implemented, and the Delors Plan for European monetary union had already been advanced.

Chancellor Kohl, like former chancellor Konrad Adenauer, was genuinely committed to the European idea and to the primacy of the Franco-German connection. Precisely because Germany risked being perceived as bigger and more threatening, the need to be moored to Europe and anointed by the French was all the greater. This gave France additional leverage in the short term. But in accelerating European construction, Mitterrand was also being faithful to himself; he was a believer in the European idea.

A French Plan for Europe?

Context and Mind-set

To examine French policy in this period requires taking into account the mind-set of the time. With the end of the cold war came a strong sense of inevitability that U.S. forces would be withdrawn from Europe. Europeans could not help being affected by the debate in the United States about the decline of U.S. power, which at the very minimum raised questions about America's future world involvement.[6] Some in France saw this prospect as an opportunity for France to realize the Gaullist program of a "European Europe." But generally speaking, the French political class was more conscious of danger than of opportunity. France feared being left alone with a strong Germany. And the prevailing opinion was that a unified Germany would be bigger and stronger, even if it took some time to fuse East and West. In security terms, therefore, the most important task was to make sure that Germany never felt the need to ensure its own security with an independent defense. Thus, if a continued U.S. presence could not be counted on, it was imperative to tie Germany to Europe through a multilateral European security system. With its nuclear weapons, France could claim some kind of leadership in such an enterprise. Besides, the prospect of U.S. withdrawal, whether viewed as a threat or an opportunity, highlighted the need for a system of European security.

At the same time, however, the belief prevailed that the real power in the world was economic. After all, it was argued, the USSR had fallen because its overextended military rested on too weak an economic base. The United States may have been the sole surviving superpower, but did it not too suffer from overextension? Germany was looked upon as well on the road to becoming a great economic power. Might it not begin a peaceful *Drang nach Osten*? As the only nation that could successfully underwrite Soviet modernization, might it develop a special relationship with the USSR, even at the expense of its erstwhile Western allies? There was much loose talk in Paris and elsewhere about Rapallo and a German *Sonderweg* (special path). And would not an economically dominant Germany begin to translate its economic power into political clout? All the more reason, in the French view, for France to quickly and irrevocably anchor Germany economically and monetarily to Western Europe while it still had some leverage.

Of course, the fear was that in such a Europe Germany would be preeminent. But from the French point of view, what was the alternative? After 40 years of trying to moor

Germany, France could not afford to entertain the notion so rife in England that it should retain a maximum degree of independence as a hedge against German resurgence. But the French certainly worried about becoming geographically peripheral, the second-rate appendage of a German Mitteleuropa (Central Europe) they themselves helped to construct. To some extent, the French quest for European monetary and political union thus began as an exercise in damage control—an effort to make a virtue of necessity.

The Gulf War marked the beginning of this shift in thinking. The old Allied coalition—the United States, the United Kingdom (UK), and France—had fought together. Germany was uncomfortably on the sidelines until it came to paying the bill. The war proved that there was still a need for military power after the cold war; it also indicated that the United States was not likely to disappear from Europe as rapidly as some had feared. Fighting in the Balkans, however unwanted, demonstrated that economic power was not enough to maintain political stability in Eastern Europe and that, with Germany still under self-limiting provisions about the exercise of military force, France's role in Eastern Europe was not negligible. Nor, with the collapse of the USSR and the extraordinary extent of Russia's problems, was it possible to imagine that any nation could assume responsibility for, and obtain the benefits of, rebuilding the Russian economy. And Germany, increasingly consumed by the gravity of its own problems, was not in a position to assert European hegemony. France continued to pursue the same European agenda but with more confidence that it was engaged in a positive program, not merely in damage control.

Process and Program

The mechanism for the process of European construction was to be two intergovernmental conferences or IGCs, one on European Monetary Union (EMU) and one on European Political Union (EPU), proposed by President Mitterrand

and Chancellor Kohl in April 1990 and convoked by the June 1990 Dublin European Council meeting. The urgency felt by France to moor Germany and by Germany to gain legitimacy for unification explain the rapid convocation of the IGCs and the relatively short time allotted to prepare a revision of the Treaty of Rome for European Council action. Joint Franco-German statements – the Kohl-Mitterrand declaration of December 6, 1990, the Dumas-Genscher working paper of February 4, 1991, and the Kohl-Mitterrand statement of October 14, 1991 – catalyzed the process and adumbrated the positions finally accepted at Maastricht.

The fact that a political decision was being made that required a complex and technical follow-through guaranteed that the general public would not pay much attention to the detailed negotiations of an arcane treaty. It may be that the treaty could only have been negotiated through contact between a small number of key players. But these players had little sense that there could be a political price to pay when hitherto uninvolved parliaments or publics were called upon to ratify what they had negotiated.

The process of negotiations was nearly ignored not only by the French public but by the political class as well, principally because it was overshadowed by events in the Gulf and appeared quixotic when juxtaposed with Europe's inchoate response there. Moreover, Franco-German negotiations took place behind closed doors – the work of a small number of people operating from the Elysée, the Quai d'Orsay, and the Bundeskanzleramt, with only limited contact with the relevant ministries. Such texts and declarations as were made public could be dismissed as "theater," while private discussions remained private. Add to this the pervasive skepticism about Mitterrand's commitment to Europe and understandably the Kohl-Mitterrand declaration, for example, was not accorded much attention.

France's strategy was to work with Germany to build Europe by engaging in a broad process of coalition-building. Like de Gaulle, when the current French president wanted to know what France thought, he "interrogated himself." During the negotiations, Mitterrand himself could speak for France. But the task of a German chancellor was more difficult. He could not make major policy decisions without knowing that he had the support of his party, the foreign minister, and the Bundesbank. And because the Treaty of Rome was to be revised, Social Democratic Party (SPD) votes were required in the Parliament. Both French and Germans recognized that to develop a joint position required working closely with the European Commission, especially with Commission president Jacques Delors. They also realized that it would be dangerous should a common Franco-German position look to other European states like a fait accompli or diktat. The French and Germans had to continue to work with the Italians, try to include the British, and soothe the wounded feelings of the Dutch.

Historically, when French and Germans agreed among themselves, they could bring along with them most of the continental EC members. But French officials nevertheless spoke repeatedly of avoiding the experience of the Fouchet Plan of 1961–1962—that is, of giving the impression of wanting to foist a fully developed French (in this case Franco-German) plan on a recalcitrant Community.[7] Finally, in the process of coalition-building, the position of the United States had to be taken into account, at least in the area of security. The result would be a complex document that respected the needs of national and party leaders of 12 countries, but not of European public opinion, which was not seen as a player in the process.

What kind of Europe did the French want? In an unpublished paper on "France in the New Europe," Nicole Gnesotto, deputy director of the WEU's Institute for Security Studies, argued that the Kohl-Mitterrand statement envisioned a Europe that is federalist for economic and monetary questions, but intergovernmental in the political, foreign policy, and security domains. France and Germany's commitment to significant deepening of the EC was most opposed by the United Kingdom. Paris and Bonn's interest in developing a security dimension to the treaty also met the most resistance from the UK and the Netherlands, which were concerned about the possible impact on NATO. The Netherlands (which held the European Council presidency during the second half of the IGCs), on the other hand, would have preferred a greater role for supranational, rather than intergovernmental, authority. Where France and Germany differed most was on the democratic deficit.

The French position on EC institutions attached verbal significance to the notion of a "federalist vocation" but, in practice, emphasized the centrality of the European Council. The term "federalism" was not employed in the classic Monnet sense, although just using the term "federalist" seemed daring enough at the time. In the words of Elisabeth Guigou, junior minister in charge of European affairs, to the National Assembly on December 12, 1990, "We say, with a federalist vocation because we consider that we cannot immediately make a federal constitution, but we are engaged in that direction." What characterized the French démarche was an unremitting emphasis on the importance of strengthening the European Council. As Madame Guigou put it:

> Our concern is to go as far ahead as possible, especially in matters of foreign policy. . . . Since we don't think it possible, in the course of the coming years, to delegate to a supranational organism powers which at present belong to heads of state and heads of government, it appeared necessary to us to base ourselves on the institution which already makes all the great decisions, the European Council.[8]

Considerations of efficacy were not the only reasons for this position. France, as one of the few old centralized European states, has been reluctant to abandon political sovereignty. As European affairs ceased to be questions of foreign policy and became matters of day-to-day business, they fell from the Elysée to the purview of Brussels or the Matignon. Through the European Council, the president of the republic could recuperate on the European level some of the powers thus lost. Perhaps Mitterrand was more concerned about correcting the "national executive deficit" than the "democratic deficit." The Germans, less enamored of the European Council than the French and more concerned about the democratic deficit, did not, however, stand in the way of a ringing endorsement in the Kohl-Mitterrand declaration of December 6, 1990.

The Kohl-Mitterrand declaration proposed, vaguely enough, to deal with the "democratic deficit" issue by reinforcing the co-decision powers of the Parliament for "truly legislative actions" and by giving it the right to confirm the president of the Commission and ultimately all Commission members. The Germans showed more interest than the French in increasing the role of the Parliament. Indeed, strengthening the European Parliament was held up as a precondition for ratification of the treaty not only by the Bundestag but by the Italian Parliament as well. Yet the German government did not fight very hard to increase the powers of the European Parliament, nor did the German Parliament live up to its threat of refusing ratification. The German government experienced pressure from the Länder, or German states, who wanted a say in Brussels. Lack of Franco-German agreement explains the laconic reference in the declaration to "associating the national parliaments more tightly to the union and how the regions can make their interests felt on the essential questions which concern them." The Kohl-Mitterrand statement left to the intergovernmental conferences this thorny issue, which was not far advanced by the treaty.

The two most difficult issues that faced the negotiations were the EMU and European security—in other words, the balance of the mark and the bomb. It is of singular importance that the results of the two intergovernmental conferences were to be ratified as a package.

For Mitterrand, Kohl, and Delors, the EMU was above

all a political accomplishment – the logical completion of the Single European Act and the culmination of the economic integration of the European Community. The idea was not new, nor was it initially tied to German unification. The Delors Plan of April 1989 had already outlined a three-step plan for monetary union, but German unification acted as its catalyst. The European Monetary System (EMS) was to be transformed into a single currency. At the time, the idea seemed feasible, because the EMS had been working well for the previous decade, at least for the stronger currencies.

Except for the British, who were never enthusiastic about the idea, the question was not whether the EMU would work or whether it would be in the mutual interest of all European nations, but how to work out the modalities. To the extent that the Bundesbank was already a de facto Eurofed or European central bank, France had nothing to lose by creating a Eurofed over which it would have some influence, whereas it had none on the Bundesbank.[9] Besides, the French had made a virtue of following German economic and monetary policy and at most would want a somewhat greater tilt toward economic growth.

Critics claimed that the EMU would make it impossible for the French state to follow its own economic and monetary policies, but for a decade France's policies had been identical to those of Germany. In Germany, the Bundesbank was far from enthusiastic about ceding power to a European central bank. Thinking in economic and not political terms, it insisted on the full independence of the Eurofed, on economic convergence among EMU members, and on applying the Bundesbank's monetary principles to the new central bank. Mitterrand and Kohl both resisted opposition to the EMU within their nations, but the timetable for reaching the third stage of the EMU was lengthened and the role of the European Monetary Institute in the second stage limited.

One reason that the Franco-German blueprint came through the negotiations largely unscathed was that

France and Germany were able to carry many other European states with them. Great Britain, the country least happy about much of the Franco-German plan, undermined its influence by seeking to opt out of the EMU and the social charter. It used up political capital to eliminate the word "federalist vocation" from the document—a Pyrrhic victory.

Enlargement

To understand the French view of the future of Europe requires examining the French attitude toward issues related to EC enlargement. Although not on the agenda of the IGCs, enlargement could not be forgotten. What were the boundaries of Europe? What was the relationship of deepening to widening? In particular, how should the EC deal with the problem of Eastern Europe? These were important questions that provoked tension between France and Germany.

The liberation of Eastern Europe came at a time when the United States was unwilling to take the lead in providing economic assistance to Europe as it did after World War II with the Marshall Plan. This left Western Europe with primary responsibility. But Western Europe did not believe it had the resources for a program of such magnitude. Presumably the status of Eastern Europe would be resolved eventually by full membership in the EC. Until then, the EC could enter into association agreements with these countries, agreements that would hold out the hope, but not the guarantee, of full membership.

Treaties with Czechoslovakia, Hungary, and Poland did not include provisions for completely free trade or free movement of persons. The problem in trade negotiations was EC reluctance to include agriculture, steel, and textiles, areas in which it had its own surplus. But agriculture and low-tech industrial products are precisely the kind of items that a nation like Poland produces. These agreements also did not provide for free movement of populations. Thus, even in the short term, the problem became what economic sacrifices the Community was willing to make for political returns. The answer was not obvious and negotiations were rocky. Concern about French agricultural interests even prompted France to block these agreements temporarily in September 1991 over the subject of meat imports.

But Eastern Europe not only constituted a problem for the European Community as a whole. The states of Western Europe operate both as part of the EC and as nation-states, thus viewing Eastern Europe from both perspectives. The classical conflicts over power between West European nation-states were sublimated into struggles for influence. Eastern Europe became the locus of one such struggle.

The basic problem was that German unification had upset the balance within the EC. It seemed there were no longer any political barriers to German economic expansion in the East. More than any other West European state, Germany saw its security closely tied to Eastern Europe, and the Eastern states saw their fate tightly linked to Germany. At the same time, other West European nations worried about potential German economic hegemony in Mitteleuropa as did the Eastern Europeans, who wanted German presence but not dominance.

German policy toward the East in 1991 was logical and clear. First, the Germans wanted to make the most of the Council on Security and Cooperation in Europe (CSCE) to provide security guarantees for Eastern Europe. The best argument for that was the lack of alternatives; but in making a virtue out of necessity, the Germans tended to exaggerate the possibilities inherent in CSCE and legalistic solutions. One reason may have been the belief that refusal of states to obey international law would cost them EC economic assistance and the chance for future admission. This predicated behavior based on a narrowly economic view of rational self-interest.

Second, Germany wanted to foster an economically and politically stable Eastern Europe and tried to push forward EC association agreements to help Poland, Czechoslovakia, and Hungary make the economic transition within the 10-year time frame of the agreements. At that point, Germany hoped, if at all economically possible, to support admission of these states into the EC as stipulated in the German-Polish treaty. This would also provide a de facto guarantee of their security. The Germans cited the admission of Spain, Portugal, and Greece in the 1970s as a precedent for admitting economically marginal states for political reasons. A major reason for bolstering these states and their economies was to avoid a vast wave of immigration to Germany.

The Germans, well aware of the fears of other nations that Germany would economically dominate Eastern Europe, worried that these fears could become a self-fulfilling prophecy. Consequently, they encouraged other nations to invest there. But that is precisely the problem: the French in particular believed, rightly or wrongly, that their private sector could not compete effectively with Germany's. Volkswagen's success in taking over Skoda at the expense of Renault seemed to substantiate these fears. French policy toward the East thus sought ways of getting around the alleged problem of economic inferiority by a variety of means: engaging in bilateral relations with the Eastern nations, encouraging trade and investment and cultural influence, developing multilateral structures like the Confederation, and using Community institutions as a way of compensating for German economic strength. This policy became so tortuous that it actually may have harmed French interests.

The French were committed to the deepening, but not the imminent widening, of the Twelve—that is, they wanted a Europe with a fundamentally West European orientation. Their idea was to irrevocably shape the new European political institutions before enlargement. They feared that a Europe that expanded rapidly to include the countries in the European Free Trade Agreement (EFTA) and Eastern

Europe would be a Europe of the lowest common denominator, especially in the security domain, where many of the EFTA states are neutrals. They may also have privately feared the implications of opening up the Community to a Northern Europe that is economically and culturally close to Germany and to an Eastern Europe that could be in thrall to its powerful neighbor. Mitterrand's idea of the Confederation, bolstered by the European Bank for Reconstruction and Development (EBRD), was thus a means of keeping the nations of the East out of the EC while maintaining privileged ties with them.

Although this position was logical, it was undermined by the French desire to become the advocate of nations where political, cultural, and historical realities give France some influence, like Poland and Romania. If certain nations of the East were inevitably going to join the EC, better that France should get some of the credit. So France promised Poland and Czechoslovakia it would support their candidacies for EC membership "as soon as possible" (admittedly an ambiguous term). Thus, in practice, France seemed to be pursuing contradictory policies.

At the same time, according to Danish political scientist Ole Waever, Mitterrand emphasized a broad-based EC policy of political and economic development in Eastern Europe,

> because this is the only way to counterbalance German economic dominance in Eastern Europe. German firms act on economic reasoning to invest in Eastern Europe, and German economic expansion thus grows from laissez-faire—that is, non-state processes. French companies, on the other hand, have neither the strength nor the motives for comparable investment. Thus the less political "help" is extended to Eastern Europe, the more German economic dominance will take hold.[10]

In this context, it is easy to see why France was so firm a supporter of the concept of the EBRD.

The already complex French policy toward Eastern Europe was complicated further by the concept of the Confederation. The Confederation, first mooted in December 1989, was rooted in Mitterrand's desire to offer his own version of Gorbachev's "common European house." According to German policy analyst Ingo Kolboom, Mitterrand specifically wanted to counter the threat of the destructive forces of nationalism and to offset possible German dominance in Eastern Europe. The Confederation was intended to embed Germany in a common European structure, the main pillar of which was the EC but to which Eastern Europe would be bound by a confederal relationship.[11] The persistence of the idea, which never aroused much enthusiasm within or without France, can only be explained by the French president's obstinacy.

Murky at best, the Confederation provoked opposition any time it went beyond the realm of metaphor to more concrete proposals. The Americans were angered at not being among the countries included, the Germans were concerned that it interfered with CSCE, and the Eastern Europeans wanted nothing to do with any organization that not only threatened their ties with the United States but seemed to stand in the way of EC membership. President Mitterrand's radio statement of June 12, 1991, suggesting that it would take tens and tens of years before the countries of the East could join the EC, guaranteed the virtual failure of what was supposed to be the founding meeting of the Confederation June 12–14, 1991, in Prague.

The fundamental tension within the Confederation was between its title — which is political and juridical — and its content, which the Quai d'Orsay tried to tie to concrete projects of cooperation between European states in the areas of energy, environment, transportation, communication, and culture (areas in which France believes it has some special assets). Perhaps the Confederation would have lost any of its political and juridical meaning had not Mitterrand resisted. But it was precisely the issues raised by the political-juridical aspect that angered then Czechoslovak president Vaclav Havel and caused problems in Prague.

Far from having been a triumph of French diplomacy, as Mitterrand intended, the meeting called attention to the internal contradictions of French policy that Mitterrand himself exacerbated. The situation was aggravated when, for reasons of domestic politics in a preelectoral period, the French briefly blocked trade concessions to Poland, Czechoslovakia, and Hungary to protect French farmers, despite European consensus in the post-Soviet coup period on the need to conclude these agreements rapidly. Mitterrand's own actions unwittingly undermined French influence in Eastern Europe, thereby increasing the very danger of German dominance they sought to avert.

But Western Europe's policy debate over Eastern Europe was not only tied to the political and economic balance of power in the New Europe. It was also tied to its socioeconomic character. Clearly, the end of the cold war confirmed and accelerated the decline of communism in Western Europe. There was no longer a communist model for Western Europe, let alone for Eastern Europe. But there was no socialist blueprint for Europe either. Since the French Socialist Party's failed effort to "change life" in 1981–1983, no one anywhere has attempted to articulate a democratic socialist alternative to free market ideology. That is not to say that European socialists and social democrats, including Mitterrand and Delors, accepted Thatcherism. Nor is the kind of free market economics found in Anglo-Saxon countries the same as "social market" economics in continental Europe. The question of an industrial policy, especially as a means of countering the Japanese challenge, was still alive. The battle thus continued as to the nuances of the future political economy of the EC, a battle that began more than 40 years ago. In 1964, George Lichtheim wrote:

> The extent to which public ownership and planning of the economy are compatible with the operation of the

> market economy cannot be determined beforehand,
> and the debate thus gives rise to serious divergencies;
> but in principle all parties concerned are aware that it
> is a question of balance, not of substituting one social
> order for another.[12]

This was still largely true. But the debate over balance informed West European attitudes toward how to help the East and the nature of the desired outcomes there, for what the East becomes and how it gets there will affect the nature of an enlarged EC as well.

The European Bank for Reconstruction and Development, a French-inspired program first headed by one of Mitterrand's closest protégés, Jacques Attali, was clearly intended by the French to encourage development in the East by supporting infrastructure development as well as to promote the Confederation. But free market supporters saw these policies, with considerable truth, as supporting a more statist economic model than they themselves favor. This was hardly surprising; France has always worked to create an EC whose institutions would retain many of the statist aspects of the French economy.

The signing of the Maastricht Treaty seemed to have resolved the question of enlargement in the sense the French desired. Maastricht would provide for the deepening of the Community, including the security dimension. Enlargement would take place only afterward. New members would not dilute the consensus but rather have to sign onto it. But the aftermath of Maastricht called into question many of the assumptions about the future of Europe described in this chapter.

2

Security

The perceived need to advance a program for monetary and political union intensified in the face of German unification. As such, it was yet another stage in resolving one of the two great issues facing France after World War II—how to achieve reconciliation with Germany. Since 1950, this issue has been addressed primarily within the context of European institutions.

But the problem of German unification had a security dimension as well, which related it to the second major problem facing postwar France—how to achieve a balance between France's desire to guarantee its own security and its need to be part of a multilateral structure dominated by the United States. The end of the cold war and German unification, the passing of what the French called the "Europe of Yalta," required the French to reevaluate their policy on European security and by implication their relationship with the United States, to find a new equilibrium between national independence, European cohesion, and Atlantic solidarity.

Since de Gaulle, France has been the most vocal West European critic of U.S. views on European security and the most conspicuous dissenter within the Atlantic Alliance. After the cold war, France supported the movement of the

European Community into the areas of security and defense and became the main proponent of a more autonomous European security role through the Western European Union.

French security policy is marked by continuity. Long-term historical factors, not short-term considerations, determine the way France conducts its defense policy. This chapter examines the premises on which French defense policy rests. It then discusses developments in French security policy directly after the cold war ended and German unification took place.[1]

Foundations of French Security Policy

France as Nation-State

The fundamental cause of Franco-U.S. discord on security issues is a difference in perceiving the nature of international relations in the postwar era. During the cold war, the United States believed that it was acting not simply out of self-interest, but as the disinterested champion of the West. France, alone of U.S. allies, continued to articulate its foreign policy in terms of national interest. It so firmly believed this to be a universal norm that it assumed any state that claimed to be acting for "higher" motivations was being hypocritical. (This clash in style recalls the mutual incomprehension of U.S. president Woodrow Wilson and French premier Georges Clemenceau at Versailles.) The French thought the United States was aiming at hegemony; the United States saw the French as troublemakers and cynics. But these differences in *perception* in turn are grounded on different *historical experiences*:

* *Unlike the other nations of postwar Western Europe, France continued to conceive of itself almost entirely in traditional nation-state terms.*

France is a highly centralized state that has long been conscious of its national identity. The defense of national interest through foreign policy and the military means of executing foreign policy is considered an inherent attribute of national sovereignty. This is hardly an idiosyncratic concept. It was the norm in Europe before World War II. But the war dramatically affected Italian and German values. The dictatorial state of Mussolini gave way to a weak state that abandoned the desire to play a major role in global politics. It happily subsumed its policies in those of NATO and the EC.

Germany acquired an allergy against the use of force as an instrument of foreign policy, sought its identity within European and Atlantic multilateral structures, and until unification found the very term "national interest" disquieting. Neither of the World War II victors—the British and the French—lost faith in the legitimacy of force in international affairs (indeed the experience of appeasement strengthened belief in its necessity). But the United Kingdom saw itself as the junior partner of the United States, exercising its influence within the "special relationship." Suez eliminated any willingness to go it alone. The same humiliation over Suez had the opposite effect on France, demonstrating not that France should abandon its international role but that it needed the means to maintain its freedom of action. Defeat in colonial struggles in Indochina and Algeria only reinforced its determination to play a global role. One reason de Gaulle sacrificed French Algeria was because it stood in the way of France's exercising its international influence.[2]

• *French historical experience contributes a mixed legacy of feelings of grandeur and insecurity.*

France's history helps explain its sense of its own greatness. On two occasions, during the reigns of Louis XIV and Napoleon, France verged on hegemony in Europe. In addition, during much of the modern period, Paris has been the great cultural capital of Europe. But at other times, before 1648 and after 1870, France went through periods of dangerous isolation and desperately sought al-

lies against the Hapsburgs and then the Germans. France's
fundamental insecurity has often been masked in the rhetoric of grandeur or mistaken for a desire for grandeur. For
example, the British erroneously construed France's hard-
line diplomacy after World War I as a desire to dominate
the continent; in reality, it was based on a pessimistic (and
accurate) assessment of France's weakness compared with
the latent strength of Germany.

   • *France has manifested ambivalence in desiring allies
but fearing dependency.*

   France's experience after 1870 demonstrated how important allies were, but its experience after 1918 proved
how dangerous it was to rely on them. After all, the United
States, which had promised to enter into a military conven-
tion with France and the UK after World War I reneged
because of Senate opposition; the UK then refused guarantees as well. The United States and the UK opposed and
helped sabotage the Ruhr occupation of 1923, which was
France's last effort at independent military action to con-
strain Germany in the interwar period.[3] In the postwar era,
the United States also torpedoed the Suez operation and
was not supportive on Algeria. Thus, the French learned
from history that they needed to be able to defend themselves, that in no case should an alliance lead to dependence
on others for national defense or justify the elimination of
a national capacity for self-defense or decision making. The
French National Assembly defeated the European Defense
Community Treaty in 1954 not only because it feared German rearmament (German rearmament was inevitable and
the Assembly shortly thereafter accepted the Treaty of
London) but because it feared eliminating the autonomy of
the French army.[4]
   France, then, has had a "Gaullist" tradition independent of the existence of Charles de Gaulle. De Gaulle gave
radical expression to broadly accepted French principles.
(On the other hand, had de Gaulle not established the

French resistance movement Free France in 1940 or returned to power in 1958 France might not have remained a significant or independent European state.) How then did de Gaulle's tenure as president specifically affect French security policy?

The De Gaulle Difference

De Gaulle accepted the reality of the cold war but was convinced that it was a transient phenomenon. For de Gaulle, the world was composed of nation-states. He believed it unnatural for countries to suppress national interest in the name of ideology. While recognizing the necessity of Atlantic cooperation – especially at times of genuine military tensions – he anticipated (and worked to create) the breakdown of both Eastern and Western blocs and return to a "normal" international situation in which each nation recovered its independence. He anticipated the reunification of Germany.[5]

De Gaulle distrusted the United States, in large part because of his wartime experience. He was convinced that the United States had wanted to eliminate him from leadership of France during the war in part because he rejected President Franklin Roosevelt's postwar vision of the end of empires and assumptions concerning U.S. dominance. The fact that the British put themselves under U.S. leadership persuaded him that the UK had become an American Trojan horse in Europe.

De Gaulle's "certain idea of France" required that France remain a great power. He distrusted the structure of NATO, which seemed to enshrine Anglo-American dominance and French inferiority. France should not be subject to a military command over which it had no political control. For de Gaulle, it was logical to remain a member of the North Atlantic Alliance but not of the integrated military command. France would control its own destiny: it would be free to decide if and when it would fight.

The possession of nuclear arms would restore France's

rank as a great power and its freedom of action. It decreased the possibility that France would be drawn into a war not of its own choosing or be abandoned in case the United States hesitated to reply to a Russian attack on Western Europe. In practice, France continued to benefit from the U.S. nuclear umbrella while increasing its freedom of action.

De Gaulle wanted a Europe sufficiently strong to play an independent role internationally but not one in which the sovereignty of its member states was significantly reduced. In fact, both de Gaulle and Monnet's conceptions of Europe were contradictory. Monnet strongly supported a supranational Europe but, remembering that it was the United States that saved Europe twice from Germany, advocated Atlantic ties and U.S. leadership. De Gaulle, who opposed supranationalism and who had thrown the Common Market into crisis when he opposed strengthening its central authority, nevertheless wanted Europe to play a foreign policy role much larger and more independent from the United States – "l'Europe européenne."

The key to de Gaulle's European policy was Germany. The Franco-German relationship would be the motor force of European political cooperation, which de Gaulle hoped to implement by intergovernmental means under the Fouchet Plan, proposed in 1961. When the Dutch and Belgians, who disliked France's disregard for federalism and feared de Gaulle's desire to establish a European political identity against the United States, vetoed the Fouchet Plan, de Gaulle pushed for closer bilateral ties with Germany, including in the security domain. These ties were embodied in the Elysée Treaty of 1963. But after the Bundestag attached a preamble emphasizing that nothing in the treaty should be seen as denying the primacy of NATO and once Adenauer was replaced as chancellor by the Atlanticist Ludwig Erhard, France was relatively isolated.

During the 1960s, East-West tensions were too great and the Soviet military threat too serious for Europe to abandon the U.S. nuclear umbrella. De Gaulle tried to force Bonn to choose between Paris and Washington. Bonn resented being asked to choose – not for the last time.

De Gaulle anticipated a rapid end to East-West confrontation and the dissolution of the two blocs. The Sino-Soviet split seemed a harbinger of such changes, but the Soviet invasion of Czechoslovakia in 1968 indicated that de Gaulle was too optimistic. This Soviet action undermined de Gaulle's foreign policy almost as much as May 1968 undermined his political legitimacy. De Gaulle's successors confronted a Soviet bloc that showed little sign of collapse. On the contrary, it seemed frankly expansionist in the Third World and unwilling to tolerate significant change in Eastern Europe. By 1981, when François Mitterrand was elected president, it seemed as if the military balance in Europe was shifting against the West.

De Gaulle succeeded in imposing many of his basic ideas on even his most bitter political opponents, including Mitterrand. The Fifth Republic's constitutional structure ceased to be an issue, and a foreign policy consensus, based on maintaining an independent national defense, emerged in the late 1970s. But it was impossible to ignore the Soviet threat, especially during the INF debate, and conduct French defense policy as if NATO did not exist or was not relevant. Thus, the history of French defense policy after de Gaulle's departure involved a process of de facto rapprochement with the United States and NATO on an operational level, accompanied by public manifestations of independence, mostly on the declaratory and symbolic level, and often especially galling to the United States. Once French-German relations improved under Giscard d'Estaing and West Germany's Helmut Schmidt, the Germans, who wanted to remain close to both Washington and Paris, usually sought to achieve cooperation between their two allies. The idea of a French return to NATO's unified military command, however, never was realistic. De Gaulle's successors were left to work out the fundamen-

tal ambivalence of Gaullist policy toward the United
States and NATO and the tension between France's desire
for independence and European identity.[6]

The Mitterrand Record

In these areas of French ambivalence, it fell to François
Mitterrand to make key choices. His decisions during the
cold war and before German unification were predicated
largely on his assessment of the Soviet threat and the status of Germany. Mitterrand's attitude toward the Soviet
Union was far more negative than that of his predecessors
as president; he did not try to play the "Soviet card." Indeed, by the time he became president, the philocommun-
ism of the intellectuals had been reversed. More important,
however, Mitterrand believed the Soviet threat had increased. Unlike Giscard d'Estaing, he did not minimize the
invasion of Afghanistan or the declaration of martial law
in Poland—his reaction was closer to that of U.S. President
Ronald Reagan. He was alarmed at the buildup of SS-20s
and supported U.S. deployment of the INF in Western
Europe. In short, taking seriously the Soviet threat dic-
tated rapprochement with the United States. But this
same issue of INF deployment also affected his policy toward Germany.

Mitterrand was worried about shaky German support
for INF deployment, especially the SPD's opposition after
Schmidt's downfall. Not only was Mitterrand concerned
about the reality of the Soviet threat, but he shared the
traditional French desire that Germany be moored. The
French did not want Germany embarked on a *Sonderweg*.
They feared Germany's appeasing Moscow to maintain fa-
vorable ties with the GDR and Eastern Europe or ultimately returning to a purely national defense. Mitterrand,
leader of a nation that was an à la carte member of NATO,
did not want Germany as an à la carte member of the
alliance. Just as the French had difficulty understanding
the United States, they had difficulty understanding Ger-

many. Seeing the Germans in French terms, they assumed that Germany would make use of its economic power to achieve political leadership. They could not believe that the Germans were not secretly obsessed with reunification. This explains French tenacity in wanting to bind Germany to Europe multilaterally and to France bilaterally.

In short, Mitterrand's policy can be characterized as both more Atlanticist and more European than his predecessors'. Mitterrand's policies presupposed a world in which the fundamentals remained stable and change was incremental: the cold war would go on, the alliance with the United States would remain necessary, European construction would continue. France would increase its cooperation with NATO but remain independent from the integrated military command; the rough "balance of the bomb and the mark" that characterized Franco-German relations would endure. The events of 1989–1991 radically altered these assumptions; France confronted the end of the cold war, German unification, the Gulf War, and the breakup of the Soviet Union.

Initially the French elite reacted to German unification with panic (as opposed to the supportive reaction of the general public). Mitterrand's irritation with a situation that had gone beyond his control explains his decision to withdraw French troops from Germany – in a fit of pique. But within several months, the government put together a program consistent with French policy toward Germany since the Schuman Plan. The idea – to moor a unified Germany by deepening the EC – was quite feasible, given a strongly pro-European German government. As noted in the previous chapter, the Dublin Summit of the EC in June 1990 agreed to hold two intergovernmental conferences on economic and monetary union and political union, which culminated in the Maastricht summit. The process of mooring would also take place on the security level.

Believing that the United States might not remain indefinitely in Europe and fearing above all a German return to national defense, the French wanted to create a framework for European security to which Germany would be tied. Because this system would be related to the EC, the EC would have to develop a security dimension. Such a system would counter the danger of a unilateral German defense should the United States disengage from Europe but could also be used to encourage a "reform" of NATO in directions desired by France.

The Kohl-Mitterrand statement of December 6, 1990, addressed to the president of the European Council, asserted that "foreign policy and common security would have the vocation of extending to all areas" and "that political union should include a genuine security policy that would lead in the end to a common defense." The text proposed that "the conference study how the WEU and the political union could establish a clear and organic relation and how consequently the WEU, rendered more operational, could eventually be part of the political union and draw up for that political union a common security policy." It added, "We are convinced that the Atlantic Alliance as a whole would be reinforced by the increase in the role and responsibilities of the Europeans and by the constitution in its midst of a European pillar."[7] The WEU was the chosen instrument for security cooperation, not only because it already existed but because turning to the WEU made it possible to finesse the problem that not all EC members could or would take part in a common security policy. Ireland was neutral, as were some potential new members.

Discussion progressed during January and February, propelled by the unfolding logic of the Kohl-Mitterrand process and the intergovernmental conferences, the degrading situation in the Soviet Union, which demonstrated that the security threat from the East had not disappeared, and the difficulty of formulating an effective European role in the Gulf. For European security and defense, the French wanted a distinct, institutionalized, and visible role with a military component. For the Germans, the sine qua non for the creation of a European security system was that it not be seen as an effort to exclude the United States. Germany, as well as other nations, wanted to be sure that French projects to create a European security system would not, wittingly or unwittingly, trigger a U.S. departure from Europe. The United States, uneasy about the idea of a European security system, was not unwilling to play upon these fears.

The Dumas-Genscher "Joint Initiative on establishing a common European foreign and security policy" of February 4, 1991, was predicated on the acceptance of NATO, although the French clearly were talking about a restructured NATO. It foresaw a WEU that would become the nucleus of a European defense entity but at the same time serve as the European pillar of NATO, thereby reinforcing the alliance. The document called for the development of a Common Foreign and Security Policy embracing all areas of foreign relations, which would eventually open up the prospect of a common European defense. An organic relationship would be developed between the European Union and the WEU. The European Union would determine the directives and guidelines for the common foreign and security policy, which would be respected by the WEU.[8] The French here would have preferred stronger language explicitly placing the WEU under European Council aegis. They did not accept the notion that the WEU would exercise its role only in out-of-area conflicts.

There are several reasons why Germany supported this proposal. First, it was consistent with the kind of closer European political unity that Chancellor Kohl advocated in exchange for the EMU. Second, the CDU (Christian Democratic Union) believed that the only way to successfully amend (or interpret) the German constitution to permit German participation in out-of-area conflicts or in Central and Eastern Europe was through participation in a European force. Third, the Germans continued to hope that they could use this proposal to draw the French into closer cooperation with NATO. While this discussion was taking place, the crisis in the Gulf finally resulted in a war with Iraq, in which France and the United Kingdom made a significant contribution that affected the debate on European security.

Implications of the Gulf War

The Gulf War had striking consequences for France. It brought success by enabling France to restore its luster as a world power and as an active ally of the United States and UK; to reassert its *rang* (status) as a world power, after a period when conventional wisdom held that economic growth rather than military power would be decisive in the post–cold war era. France was willing to break old Gaullist taboos, placing its troops under U.S. command and allowing B-52s to use a base in southern France. French policy remained closely tied to American during the war, and in the immediate postwar period, Mitterrand made several speeches strongly praising the United States. Significantly, Franco-U.S. cooperation produced virtually no adverse domestic French reaction. The French were signaling that the French concept of a European pillar was not intrinsically anti-American. Perhaps this partly explains why one high official in the German Chancellery said at the time that he was astonished by the non-negative attitude of Britain to the Dumas-Genscher paper. This cordial understanding did not last long, however.

The war also served as a warning by confronting the French, who had focused their efforts on nuclear dissuasion, with the need to adjust their military priorities by improving conventional forces and upgrading their intelligence capabilities at a time of shrinking budgets. France's difficulty in mustering even a relatively small force to fight in the Gulf (it was not politically advisable to use conscripts, which would have required further legislative action) suggested that France could exercise great power status only as part of Western Europe, which in practice meant the need for eventual German participation. At the same time, Germany's inability to act effectively helped exorcise French fears of a dominant Germany and reinforced French claims to its own world power status and its UN Security Council seat.

Europe's failure to act more coherently was seen by the French not so much as failure but as a demonstration of the need to make greater progress in political cooperation.

The Debate on European Security Continues

What followed after the Gulf War were some forlorn attempts at Franco-U.S. rapprochement and an almost predictable series of thrusts and parries between France and the United States, accompanied by bilateral Franco-German and German-U.S. declarations. The Genscher-Dumas statement was soon followed by a strong ("raw" was the way some French and Germans described it) U.S. démarche, the so-called Bartholomew Memorandum of February 22, 1991, warning the Europeans of the dangers of damaging NATO on the eve of a key WEU meeting.

Meanwhile, however, the Gulf War was going on, and Franco-U.S. cooperation was reaching a new high. On March 14, 1991, Presidents Bush and Mitterrand met on Martinique in what appeared to be a cordial, if not idyllic, atmosphere. French foreign minister Roland Dumas declared that France's "Arab Policy" had been based on "illusions" (*Washington Post*, March 14, 1991). France made it clear that it would not complicate U.S. efforts at establishing a Middle East peace conference. Claire Tréan, *Le Monde*'s diplomatic correspondent, noted the following day that this meeting "sealed the renunciation of the dogma according to which France did not exist on the international scene without systematically taking its distances from Washington." At the same time, Mitterrand insisted that the idea of a system of European defense and NATO were not incompatible. In a *Le Monde* article the next day

(March 16), Tréan pointed out the similarity of this con-
clave with what had happened at a previous meeting with
Bush at Key Largo, where "Mitterrand congratulated himself about the apparent openness of his interlocutor, and
then had to change his tune several months later."

In any case, the honeymoon did not last long. The British proposal for a NATO Rapid Reaction Force was seen
by the French as an effort conceived in cahoots with the
Americans to stymie Franco-German efforts. But then,
once again, at the Copenhagen summit of NATO in June
the French thought that understanding had been reached
with the United States about the compatibility of NATO
and the idea of a system of European defense tied to the
EC. After all, Dumas declared, NATO was "real" while the
European system was still "virtual" (Le Monde, June 8,
1991). At the same time, the French opposed efforts by
NATO to create a partnership with the countries of the
East as part of its general opposition to changing the mission of NATO without a "real reform." The idea of the
North Atlantic Cooperation Council, announced by U.S.
secretary of state James Baker and German foreign minister Hans-Dietrich Genscher in October, was opposed by the
French, but this opposition was muted, probably because
of German support for the idea and because Germany was
also supporting another proposal dear to the French,
which was announced shortly afterward.

As discussions continued on European Political Union,
Kohl and Mitterrand launched the text of a draft treaty on
common foreign and security policy on October 14, 1991.
This text stated that the EC "will implement a common
foreign and defense policy that will eventually include a
common defense." A clear organic tie would be created between the European Union (EU) and WEU, and a permanent WEU planning staff would also be established. The
text ended by stating that "Franco-German military cooperation will be reinforced beyond the existing brigade. The
reinforced Franco-German units could thus become the ba-

sis for a European corps that could include the forces of other member states of the WEU. This new structure could also become the model for closer military cooperation between the member states of the WEU."

The Kohl-Mitterrand statement thus contributed to the ongoing discussion leading to Maastricht as well as raising the new proposal for the corps. It was also a means of pulling Mitterrand's chestnuts out of the fire for his decision to withdraw French forces from Germany. These forces could now stay in Germany as part of the corps. What was undecided at the time was whether German troops would be located in France (other than the command that would be in Strasbourg), the exact relationship of the forces to NATO, and the participation of forces from other WEU members. On April 22, the German Defense Ministry announced that joint naval maneuvers would be held in the Mediterranean in May 1992. This would be on an experimental basis and would not be part of the Franco-German corps.

The U.S. reaction was predictably wary. At the NATO summit in Rome, "President Bush challenged his European allies . . . to state clearly whether they wanted America to withdraw from Europe's defense." At the same time, Secretary of State James Baker was quoted as calling the dispute a "red herring." "The disparity between the remarks made publicly by Baker and those made privately by an Administration official suggested to reporters familiar with Administration tactics that Mr. Bush had sought, through news leaks, to manipulate their allies into protestations of support cutting through their own ambiguities" (*New York Times*, November 8, 1991). Nevertheless, the NATO summit marked the first recognition by NATO of a European security system.

If the United States was wary of the Franco-German corps, the French were equally wary of an expansion of NATO's mission. Paris saw such expansion as weakening NATO militarily and as a U.S. effort to maintain its old dominance. France was decidedly unhappy at the creation of the North Atlantic Cooperation Council (NACC). As Nicole Gnesotto pointed out in his previously cited article:

> The French do not consider the European continent as one unique space where one has to build one single order. If there is to be a new European architecture, it will be a baroque one, with several roles and institutions overlapping different tasks and missions. *But at the same time, France gives a clear priority to the Western European construction* . . . [emphasis added].

In the words of French ambassador to the United States Jacques Andréani in a speech to the Chicago Council on Foreign Relations on March 25, 1991:

> The strengthening of security in Europe in the new circumstances calls, not for a direct or indirect extension of NATO, but for the adoption of rules and procedures aimed at preventing the emergence of situations and conflicts and at finding peaceful means of settlement of these conflicts when they appear.

Andréani then referred to French proposals for a formal treaty through the CSCE, which Foreign Minister Dumas had addressed a day earlier in his speech at the opening of the CSCE meeting in Helsinki. There he supported "giving a legal form to the CSCE's commitments on security; drawing up complementary rules of behavior; seeking enhanced security guarantees of benefit to all the participating States in collaboration with the CSCE's conflict-prevention mechanism." He also advocated implementing a procedure of conciliation and arbitration.

The Maastricht Treaty included the essence of the Franco-German position on security. The EC's common foreign and security policy "shall include all questions related to the security of the European Union, including the eventual framing of a common defense policy, which might in time lead to common defense." The WEU would be an "integral part of the development of the European Union." The Union will be able to "request" the WEU to "elaborate and implement decisions and actions of the Union which have defense implications" (*Financial Times*, December 12, 1992). Thus, the Maastricht accord provided the legal framework for the kind of developments in European security and defense that France advocated.

In the aftermath of Maastricht, there were two major developments in French thinking on security and one nondevelopment. The first was Mitterrand's statement that it was time to reflect on the possibility of a European nuclear deterrent. This made it possible for French officials to speculate semiofficially on the problem of converting a national deterrent into a European deterrent. In the final analysis, a purely national deterrent is not compatible with a system of European security and defense. The second was the French moratorium on nuclear testing, which might open up discussion about including French nuclear weapons in future disarmament negotiations. The nondevelopment was the frustration of Defense Minister Pierre Joxe's desire to attend military planning meetings of NATO and meetings of NACC, apparently nixed by Dumas and Mitterrand. Joxe had stated that he did not want to be the last European minister of defense not to take part at NATO meetings (*Le Monde*, December 4, 1991). But Mitterrand turned out to be closer to de Gaulle than many "Gaullists" of the younger generation; there was a limit to what he would accept.

Reflections on Maastricht

It was commonly suggested during the Maastricht negotiations that the process of Maastricht represented a Franco-German deal in which Germany accepted monetary union (admittedly under conditions that guaranteed a solid currency, low inflation, and the independence of a Eurofed) in exchange for political union. This supposes that political union was desired more by Germany than France. Yet France clearly desired common security as much as, if not more than, Germany. And if dealing with the democratic deficit was for the Germans the cornerstone of the political union and the sine qua non for parliamentary approval, why did Germany accept a treaty that ended up by doing so little to reinforce the powers of the European Parliament?

The answer is that the central concerns of this treaty were not concrete issues – monetary union or the democratic deficit. The treaty was fundamentally a political agreement sponsored by French and German leaders equally determined to moor Germany to Europe before they passed from the scene. Monetary, political, and security union were above all *means* to achieve that political goal. And that is the way it always had been since the formulation of the Schuman Plan. Although it was obviously imprudent to try to sell the treaty as a means of mooring Germany, the complexity of the treaty made it very difficult to know how to sell the treaty at all. It was one thing to sell it to a Parliament in which a government could invoke party discipline. It was another thing to try to sell it to a whole country. And it certainly was a misfortune that Denmark was the country where it had to be sold first.

If there seemed to be a problem at the time, it was not ratification. In March 1992, I argued that the problem was that "pressure from the East will force Europe to proceed more rapidly than intended to create a common foreign policy, security and defense cooperation and the means to execute them" (*Christian Science Monitor*, March 18, 1992). But the question of ratification was not even raised.

The signing of the Maastricht Treaty concluded a remarkable chapter in French diplomacy. After initial hesitation at the time of German unification, France had made a virtue of necessity and developed a bold program to deepen the European Community in close cooperation with Germany. By assuming leadership and working with Germany, France got most of what it wanted while reinforcing

Franco-German cooperation. And although the process leading up to Maastricht began at a time when it was common to look upon France as the big loser of German unification, that perception had significantly changed after the Gulf War. In late 1991 and early 1992, the answer to the question of whether France still counted was certainly "yes." Yet only a year later, the optimistic answer to whether Europe counted was "maybe."

3

The French Plan for
Europe Unravels

"The oracles are dumb. . . . "

— Milton

The signing of the Treaty of Maastricht represented a high point for French diplomacy. France had surmounted the crisis precipitated by the end of the cold war and the unification of Germany. It had framed a new vision of European integration and together with Germany had succeeded in embodying the key elements of that vision in the Maastricht Treaty. French leaders had regained confidence that France could still play a leading role in the future of Europe and that Europe could become a coherent and powerful international actor. That the United States felt threatened by French efforts demonstrated at least France's credibility. But within a short time, the strength of European unity would be sorely tested.

The events of 1992–1993 raised questions as to whether France's ambitious plans for the New Europe were realistic. Would the New Europe turn out to be a minimalist Europe? Would the EC unravel or the setbacks to European construction prove temporary? How solid was the Franco-German couple? This chapter examines France's role in and response to the European crises of 1992–1993: the ratification of the Maastricht Treaty, the breakup of Yugoslavia, and the August 1993 failure of the European Monetary System. The French referendum on Maastricht was intended to provide new momentum for Maastricht, but instead further undermined the treaty (see chapter 4). This chapter concludes with developments of late 1993 and early 1994 that were more encouraging to French hopes for both France's role and Europe's future.

The Danish Deus ex Machina

A crisis of European confidence was set off when the Danes rejected the treaty on June 2, 1992. The Danish referendum opened up Pandora's box. By the time the Danes got around to accepting Maastricht in May 1993, it was no longer the same treaty and Europe no longer the same Europe. The Danish rejection was in part due to the uniqueness and provincialism of Denmark, a country on the periphery of Europe. Lacking strong emotional ties to the European ideal, it had entered the EC for economic reasons. But particularism and nationalism were not restricted to Denmark. Denmark itself was tangential to the future of Europe, but the Danish rejection of Maastricht was a psychological problem for Europe and a legal problem as well. Amendments to the Treaty of Rome required unanimity; either the Danes had to be brought back or else a way found to implement the treaty without them. Both could not be done simultaneously, because following the second course would prejudice the first. It was apparent, however, that if all else failed, France, Germany, and their friends would press to implement the essence of the treaty by other means. In the meantime, EC leaders devised a ratification strategy that would

• pursue the process of ratification elsewhere and then return for another vote in Denmark

• provide Denmark whatever "opt outs" it wanted so that its leaders could claim Danish interests had been taken into account

• emphasize the principle of subsidiarity – that is, decision making in the Community should take place at the lowest possible level

• demonstrate sensitivity to the parochial interests of the other 11 states, thereby endowing them with a certain capacity to blackmail the Community

• give a low profile to the Commission and its president. One reason that the Danes had rejected the treaty was the fear (partly provoked by statements emanating from Brussels) that Maastricht marked a beginning, not an end, of the transfer of power to the Community.

Although this approach succeeded in ultimately securing Danish approval, it had drawbacks. The muteness of Brussels contributed to the sense of a leadership vacuum that, at a time of increasing economic frustration, made the EC seem feckless. As a result of abandoning many aspects of the EC's program to save the treaty as a whole, there was an increasing tendency to adopt a minimalist view of the treaty, which prejudiced what the new Union could actually do if it came into being. One weakness of the treaty was that it did not appear to represent a grand idea for a New Europe to a general public that had not lived through the era of the Schuman Plan. Instead of rectifying this, European leaders scaled down the project.

The Irish "yes" of June 18, 1992, kept the treaty alive. But the road to ratification continued to be rocky. The problem was that the Danish referendum, which was resonating all over Europe, had given some national leaders pause. As a result of this popular backlash, those politicians who had opposed the treaty got a second wind. The British grasped this opportunity to weaken the treaty.

They complicated the issue by deciding to go through the ratification process only after the second Danish referendum, implying that their acceptance was contingent on that of Denmark. But most important, the Danish vote demonstrated the gap between elite attitudes and the general public, which suddenly realized that Maastricht meant more than they had expected and perhaps more than they wished.

Mitterrand's decision to hold a referendum on the treaty on September 20, 1992, was intended to demonstrate the extent of French popular support. The tepid support actually given by the French public served to undermine both the official French concept of the Community and Mitterrand's credibility in Europe and France alike. If French leaders could barely carry their own public on the idea of European union, how supportive could other European leaders be? Uncertainty about the results of the impending French referendum led to a crisis of the European Monetary System. Chapter 4 examines the impact of the referendum on the French political system. But first, how did French policy respond to the Yugoslav crisis, and how did the crisis influence France's vision of Europe?

Yugoslavia

The outbreak of the Yugoslav crisis first validated the French belief that the end of the cold war did not mean an end to security problems, that military power would still be necessary to maintain peace, and that the European Community needed an instrument for guaranteeing its security. The outbreak of fighting in summer 1991 in Slovenia and then Croatia strengthened the case for a European security plank in the Maastricht Treaty. Europe's inability to bring peace to this area, however, and its unwillingness to employ force there then undermined the credibility of the concept of a European Security and Defense Identity, of the instruments that were supposed to provide for European security, and of the European idea itself. This sense of European impotence probably increased the opposition to the Maastricht Treaty in both the Danish and French referendums.

The Yugoslav crisis and the European response have thus far gone through two stages. The first was the collapse of the Yugoslav state with the secession of Slovenia and Croatia, followed by Serb efforts at establishing a Greater Serbia by seizing Croatian territory with Serb majorities or large minorities. The second was the war in Bosnia.

In 1991, Europe, like the United States, was unwilling to accept the breakup of Yugoslavia because it threatened to destabilize the USSR (which blocked any CSCE action for that reason) and because it did not correspond with what the West saw as the interest of the region. France in particular was reluctant to accept the demise of a state it had helped to create after World War I. Once breakup seemed inevitable, Europe tended to believe violence could be avoided or controlled because of the economic and moral influence exercised by the European Community. But nationalist leaders in former Yugoslavia did not seem to be motivated by rational economic considerations or threatened by exclusion from the EC.

When the conflict began, the European response was to attempt to broker a cease-fire and negotiate a political settlement. In the event of a cease-fire, a monitoring force could be put in place. Some Europeans, at least, saw this as an opportunity to demonstrate that Europe was a political force to be reckoned with, that Europe could take care of its own problems. This occurred precisely at the time that the security provisions of the Maastricht Treaty were under discussion. When the fighting got worse, the French suggested an interposition force under the WEU. The *Financial Times* of August 8, 1991, clearly grasped France's mixed feelings:

> France . . . is seen by some as traditionally pro-Serb and opposed to German suggestions that Slovenian

and Croatian independence be recognized. This is said to be through fear of a new "Teutonic bloc" emerging, and/or to discourage its Corsican separatists.

Yet the continuing insistence of Mr. Roland Dumas, France's foreign minister, that a WEU force may eventually have to "interpose" itself in Croatia could—if carried out—greatly stengthen the Croat case for recognition. What appears overriding in the French position is its vision of Europe's defence future.

This aspect of the French posture may cause division insofar as it is seen to be prejudging the debate—unresolved within the European political union negotiations—on what sort of foreign and security policy, and eventually defence policy, the EC should have. The Yugoslav crisis itself undoubtedly strengthens the case of France and its EC allies.

The French acquiesced to Germany's desire to secure EC recognition of Croatia, trading it for German support for a September 1991 French proposal for an interposition force under the WEU. But it was precisely because of the link between this proposal and France's ambitions to strengthen the WEU vis-à-vis NATO that the UK vociferously opposed and successfully blocked creation of such a force—not just because of Britain's lack of interest in the region and unhappy experience in Northern Ireland (although these were real considerations). How serious was this proposal? Did the French offer it thinking it had a chance of being implemented or merely to demonstrate leadership? An argument for the rhetorical nature of the proposal was the lack of available forces. German troops could not participate, the United States would not be involved in a WEU operation, and France presumably could not and would not be able to mount one on its own. The UK was therefore essential, but obviously had not offered any encouragement.

The failure of the French proposal for an interposition force, the EC's consistent inability to obtain a cease-fire that was respected, and the end of the Soviet veto over involvement in Yugoslavia led eventually to the EC's hand-ing the crisis over to the UN. Although Serbia was clearly the aggressor and evidence of Serbian ambitions to create a Greater Serbia was abundant, there was no EC support for use of military force (or the threat to use military force) against Serbia, even at the time of attacks on the Croatian city of Dubrovnik. Retrospectively, some French diplomats have admitted that use of force at this point might have prevented the expansion of the conflict – but only to buttress the argument that it was now too late to use force.

The first phase of the conflict, which ended in early 1992 with a UN-supervised cease-fire in Slavonia, left open the entire territorial dispute between Serbia and Croatia. Regrettably, the end of fighting there provided an excellent opportunity for Serbian president Slobodan Milošević to turn to a "solution" of the Bosnian question. Bosnia, perhaps unwisely, had declared independence after a referendum supporting independence had been passed by a large majority, with the Bosnian Serbs, who had opposed the referendum from the beginning, boycotting the election. The outbreak of fighting was predictable – and predicted. Although recognizing the existence of Bosnia, Europe would not defend it. But Bosnia was far more vulnerable than Croatia; unlike Croatia, its very existence was threatened by Serbia. Europe once again defined its role as supporting negotiations through the UN, first with the UK's Lord Carrington and then with America's Cyrus Vance and the UK's David Owen as negotiators. It was made clear that military intervention was out of the question, thereby removing any effective limits on Serb action and undermining the prospects for a peace process. Yet the brutality of Serb forces, their policy of "ethnic cleansing," and the plight of the civilian population in Sarajevo and elsewhere made it difficult to do nothing – or at least to appear to do nothing.

As events unfolded, a contemporary observer could not fail to be struck by the lack of consistency and efficacy of French policy (not that it was more inconsistent than that of the United States or Germany). Retrospectively, it can be inferred that the main logic of French policy was to contain the conflict within Bosnia while providing humanitarian aid to the civilian population and waiting for the fighting to wind down. This was a damage-control operation. Military intervention was excluded. But at the same time, any French policy had to respond to a wide variety of conflicting pressures from both the political elite and the general public. These included

- a push for humanitarian assistance, led by Bernard Kouchner, the minister of health and humanitarian action
- the need for a common European position and recognition of the impact of the crisis on perceptions of Europe's capacity to act in defense of its own security
- a preference for solutions involving the WEU or the UN rather than NATO and a desire to demonstrate French leadership, occasionally reduced to the level of a beau geste (the Mitterrand trip to Sarajevo)
- an unwillingness, especially on the part of the French president, to break all ties to Serbia despite unhappiness with Serbian behavior
- differences of opinion between Paris and French military leaders on the ground in former Yugoslavia
- the necessity of reconciling a "realistic" view that nothing can be done because this was a tribal conflict that would take its own course with an idealistic/legalistic view that aggression cannot be recognized and rewarded
- the need to maintain good relations with the Moslem world.

These wishes could not be reconciled, resulting in a policy that seemed incapable of meeting its goals or even defining them publicly and that often changed color if not essence as a result of circumstances.

Mitterrand's dramatic flight to Sarajevo on June 28, 1992, not only sent a message of hope to the besieged population but demonstrated to French voters before the Maastricht referendum that France and Europe would not be passive spectators to the drama of Sarajevo. Mitterrand's flight did not mean, however, that France was prepared to support military intervention to save Bosnia. Instead, France supported humanitarian assistance begun under the auspices of the United Nations. The United Nations Protection Force (UNPROFOR) was to protect the humanitarian operation (and could in some indirect fashion be used to protect the Moslems), but was not there to fight. France provided the largest national contribution to UNPROFOR, which was meant to send a message about France's commitment to UN peacekeeping (and its right to a permanent seat on the Security Council). But the small scale of the UN forces as well as their limited armaments and lack of air support made them hostages to the Serbs, who treated them with scant respect. Their very vulnerability buttressed arguments against taking any military action such as bombing. But the fact that French and British forces remained essentially in the role of "hostages" for so long could also indicate that their governments were using their presence to block more energetic military intervention. According to an article by Claire Tréan and Yves Heller in *Le Monde* on November 4, 1992, the French government believed it impossible to disengage completely yet supported the UNPROFOR route because it excluded the possibility of war against Serbia.

> France did the most to get the UN to take responsibility for the Yugoslav problem, to get it to send forces and to define the completely new type of mission engaged in. But if France was the leader in all these humanitarian and political initiatives, which presumed the agreement of all parties, including the aggressor, it also constantly watched to make sure that it not go beyond this framework, and only accepted when absolutely forced the few coercive measures adopted against Serbia, resisting as much as possible.

According to Tréan, the Quai d'Orsay was privately fatalistic about the war; it would end when the Serbs got what they wanted and when the Moslems recognized that there would be no Western intervention and no lifting of the arms embargo.

The ambivalence of French policy was exemplified by the policy of "security zones," the French alternative to the U.S. proposal of "lift and strike" carried to Europe by Secretary of State Warren Christopher in May 1993:

> The French authorities had worked hard for the creation of these protected zones, an initiative by which they attempted to compensate for their renunciation of certain of the principles of the late Vance-Owen peace plan to which the Bosnian Moslems remain attached. The demarche of Paris is based on the conviction that the more the Bosnian Moslems were given the sense that one was ready to give them an international protection, the more they would be disposed to negotiate in Geneva. (*Le Monde*, July 29, 1993)

The UN took so long, however, to agree to creating these zones that sufficient forces to protect them were not found and even members of the French government did not share a common understanding of what they implied. In the summer of 1993, when the Serbs attacked French soldiers of UNPROFOR, there was no UN response. France seemed anxious to take stronger measures. At this time, the Clinton administration once again began to talk about the possibility of air strikes. Yet Defense Minister François Léotard, in Washington at the time, declared that the blue helmets in Bosnia had a humanitarian mission, that they are not in "a situation of war," and that UNPROFOR was "not there to defend Sarajevo" (*Le Monde*, August 2, 1993). As the result of a Franco-U.S. deal, the North Atlantic Assembly defined operational options for Bosnia on August 9, 1993; France considered that it had scored points by requiring that NATO intervention receive prior consent from the UN secretary general, who seemed unlikely to support it. Immediately following, on August 10, Alain Lamassoure, the new minister of European affairs, stated that use of force against the Bosnian Serbs by NATO under the authority of the UN could facilitate a diplomatic solution (*Le Monde*, August 12, 1993). In reality, the policy that prevailed was to support negotiations and, if they failed, to allow the fighting to wind down.

One of the strongest critiques of French policy came in a long and passionate article in *Le Monde* on June 17, 1993. François Heisbourg and Pierre Lellouche argued that the Yugoslav crisis was the turning point of the post–cold war era:

> What is the point of erecting heavy and complex structures like the Treaty of Maastricht, when Europeans are not even capable of acting with enough vigor to impose – if all else fails – by arms – respect for the simple principles of non-aggression and of non-expansion by force. . . . Before even being ratified, the treaty of Maastricht, and in particular . . . the sections on "foreign policy and common security" are null and bypassed by History. . . . [At the same time] the European-American alliance gives evidence of its lack of relevance . . . for the real conflicts of the post Cold War in Europe. . . .

There was a widespread sense in late 1993 that European – and French – failure in Yugoslavia sapped the credibility of the concept of a European security system, just as U.S. inaction undermined the credibility of NATO.

The Monetary Crisis and France's New German Problem

"With you or without you I cannot live."

– Ovid

If the goal of Maastricht was fundamentally political – the anchoring of unified Germany to a deepened European community – and monetary union the primary means of achieving that goal, monetary union was also seen as the final step in the movement toward economic union and as economically beneficial per se. The authors of Maastricht operated under the assumption that the economic and monetary conditions prevailing in Europe for the rest of the 1990s would resemble those of the previous 10 years. They supposed that the monetary convergence already achieved by the EMS would continue to the point that transition to a single currency would be relatively simple. These assumptions, although not implausible, were not borne out for two reasons: the deep recession experienced by Europe in the early 1990s and the fact that the Bundesbank, while functioning as the de facto central bank for all Europe, based its policy only on German interests and German interests narrowly defined, the paramount criterion being to prevent inflation rather than encourage growth.

German integration as carried out by the Kohl government proved immensely costly. The Bundesbank had opposed a 1 : 1 swap of ostmarks for deutsche marks and made the government pay for its decision. The cost of unification, however, was not directly assumed by German taxpayers but postponed through deficit spending. Fearing inflation, the Bundesbank raised interest rates and kept them high, with only minor cuts during most of 1993 as Germany moved toward recession. But with EC currencies pegged to the mark, high interest rates in Germany meant high interest rates everywhere in Europe, which posed increasingly grave problems for countries with high and growing unemployment. The tension was reflected by the tendency of large financial speculators to attack currencies that appeared overvalued.

Doubts about the outcome of the French referendum on Maastricht led to a monetary crisis in September 1992. Speculators drove the pound and lira out of the EMS; the peseta remained only through increasing the band and was devalued several times.[1] After leaving the EMS, however, Britain's economy improved. France, which had a far lower inflation rate than Germany but had high and growing unemployment, tried to lower its interest rates below Germany's. Several attacks on the franc resulted. In late July 1993, a speculative frenzy mounted that could only have been defused if the Bundesbank had lowered interest rates. When the Bundesbank refused to make the expected cut on July 29, 1993, speculators staged a massive attack on the franc. As Ian Davidson wrote in the *Financial Times* (July 31–August 1, 1993):

> From a purely economic point of view, France is obviously neglecting its real economic interests by clinging with such fierce determination to the virtually fixed exchange rate against the D-mark. But from a political point of view, the ERM at its existing exchange rates has acquired all the symbolism of the commitment to closer European integration encapsulated in the Treaty of Maastricht.

The Balladur government was not prepared to yield so long as the Bundesbank was willing to help defend the franc, as it was indeed obligated. But the attack exceeded the defense capability of the Bank of France and Bundesbank. The French government could have devalued within the band, but that would have been too little to end the attack. Allowing the franc to float would have marked an enormous loss of face and would have doomed the EMS, and probably hopes for the EMU as well. The French suggested to the Germans that they temporarily remove the mark from the EMS, which Germany appeared willing to do, but the opposition of other nations whose currencies were closely pegged to the mark foreclosed this possibility. The solution was found in temporarily increasing the fluctuation band of the EMS to 15 percent. Once this was done, pressure on the franc fell.

The French government, rather than taking the opportunity to allow a significant devaluation, continued to defend the strong franc for tactical, strategic, and political reasons. Tactically, the franc had to be kept strong while the Bank of France bought back deutsche marks for their reserves. Strategically, the government continued to support the symbolism of the franc fort (strong franc). Politically, Balladur feared the consequences of adopting the policies promoted by his strongest conservative critic, Philippe Séguin, proponent of "une autre politique." Ironically, throughout the crisis, Balladur enjoyed the support of Mitterrand and the socialists, but such support was not likely to placate his critics on the Right. This cooperation, however, was probably a precondition for the continuation of cohabitation. There was minimal support from Chirac and much opposition from within Balladur's own party, the RPR.

Ironically, little was resolved by the crisis. Many European leaders practiced a policy of denial, publicly refusing to admit the severity of the problem. But it seemed difficult to imagine how France could continue to act much longer against its immediate economic interests. The tone of the usually measured *Le Monde* in its August 3, 1993, editorial gives some sense of the anger and frustration of French elites about German policy and hints at what they were thinking and saying in private:

> All Europe today is paying for the errors committed by the government of Bonn in putting into practice the process of German unification. . . . the new Germany has made a thoughtless use of its dominant economic position on the continent. . . . the leaders of Bonn are obliged to clarify matters if they do not want the present monetary crisis to lead to the shipwreck of the entire European project.

On the next day, Jacques Lesourne, the director of *Le Monde*, speaking of Franco-German relations, asked:

> What remains, aside from institutions and a better reciprocal understanding? The two countries are neither basically in agreement on GATT nor on common trade policy, neither on enlargement nor on their attitude

towards the United States, and they are doubtless not more willing to make concessions to each other. What is the significance of an internal market with fluctuating exchanges? Why exhaust oneself to adopt directives which attempt to homogenize a fractionated economic space?

The Balladur government (just like its predecessor) had staked its survival on the franc fort despite rising unemployment in France and strong political pressures for "une autre politique," pressures that had increasing resonance in France. It was hard to overestimate the consequences for Franco-German relations of abandoning the franc fort and, with it, losing prospects for monetary union. After all, monetary union was created not only as an end in itself, but even more as a means of "mooring" a reunified Germany to Europe. Its failure would be looked upon as a decision by Germany to go its own way.

It was not only in the area of monetary policy that Franco-German relations were at a low ebb by late 1993. Germany's combination of economic power, political gridlock, and parochialism was problematic for France. In addition, Germany, having recovered its sovereignty, still continued to hold to self-singularization in the security field.

The realities of German practice undermined the finest Franco-German plans for the future of Europe. Germany supported French proposals to give Europe a security identity through the WEU and a defense potential through a Eurocorps. But these plans were largely theoretical unless German forces could be employed out-of-area. Although some CDU leaders hoped that they could alter German constitutional prohibitions on out-of-area forces by creating the Eurocorps, that had not happened.

The French were also worried about Germany's future. Although no serious analysts of Germany believed in the possibility of returning to a Bismarckian, let alone fascist, Germany, the upsurge there of racist, anti-immigrant feelings with ensuing violence, as well as rising anti-European sentiment, evoked memories of the Nazi past. The French feared that the German public was losing interest in Europe and that German elites were backing away from the EMU.

Many German officials and diplomats believed that Germany had been accommodating France for too long; now for the first time since the war they were speaking in terms of German national interests and believed it was time for France to accommodate them. As long as Helmut Kohl was chancellor, presumably, Germany would continue a pro-European policy and the Franco-German couple would remain central to German policy. But Kohl's survival as chancellor beyond 1994 was in doubt. The French worried that there would never again be another German chancellor as pro-European and pro-French as Kohl and that the Franco-German relationship could erode. And many French leaders feared the advent of an SPD-led government. Both French conservatives and socialists, uncomfortable with the defense policies of the SPD since the departure of Helmut Schmidt, prefer CDU partners, although they did show interest in new SPD leader Rudolf Scharping and his efforts to bring the SPD back to the center.

Germany and France had become privileged partners after World War II, and European cooperation hinged on their relationship. They had only two alternatives—partnership or continued conflict. Because the European context changed with the end of the cold war, French and German interests clashed more often. But both nations were extremely chary about undermining a relationship that remains the basis for European stability.

The events of 1992–1993 brought good and bad news. The good news was that the fear of a hegemonic and unilateralist Germany that had driven France to work for the rapid deepening of the EC at Maastricht had proven unreal or exaggerated. The bad news was that those events had greatly undermined the prospects for rapid movement toward further European integration.

Yet it was not the first time the EC had suffered set-

backs. Indeed, the history of the EC has been one of two
steps forward, one step back. Even if this crisis was more
fundamental than previous ones, the EC was not about to
disintegrate. The Single European Act was largely implemented. Monetary union would probably take longer than
planned. With EFTA nations awaiting entry into the EC
and many EC members anxious for them to be admitted, it
seemed likely that widening would take place before or
without significant deepening. They would be admitted before a new institutional structure that could deal effectively with 16 or 20 states rather than 12 was decided
upon. The result would not necessarily be the kind of Europe France wanted – a European superpower with coherent foreign, security, and defense policies. It risked becoming an amorphous economic unit without the will and
capacity to pursue political and security interests, a regional rather than a global player – in short, a minimalist
and inglorious Europe. Yet the French were not likely to
give up the battle.

France Resurgent?

The beginning of 1994 witnessed four developments that
improved French and European morale in late 1993 and
early 1994: Bundesbank interest rates continued to decline;
the Uruguay round concluded successfully; the French expressed satisfaction with the NATO summit; and the
United States accepted French proposals for dealing with
the Bosnia crisis. The year also began with recognition
that France might face a problem of major proportions in
North Africa.

Interest Rates, GATT, and the "New Realism"

The French became less concerned about how German interest rates would affect French unemployment and economic recovery and whether they would threaten the sta-

bility of the franc. In November 1993 the Bundesbank cut its rates in what some observers considered to be a political decision by the new Bundesbank president Tietmeyer. Tietmeyer seemed to be according greater recognition to the Bundesbank's European role and the implications of Bundesbank policy on Germany's relations with the rest of Europe. Rates continued to fall in early 1994. The decline did not guarantee that French unemployment would also fall, because much of the unemployment is based on structural causes. But at least it meant that the French would not blame the Bundesbank for the problem.

At the same time, France retained the support of the EU for its efforts to force a renegotiation of the Blair House agreement and for its stand on cultural exceptions and Airbus. Balladur was playing a high-risk game. Failure of the Uruguay round because of an inability to resolve U.S.-French differences could have adversely affected the NATO summit and all aspects of U.S.-French relations. If France had been held responsible for the failure of the General Agreement on Tariffs and Trade (GATT), the consequences for France's relations with the EU would also have been severe. A failure of Germany in particular and the EU in general to back France over GATT would have provoked a crisis with Paris. But the French, who seemed engaged in a dangerous game of brinksmanship, played their cards masterfully and obtained an agreement that pleased both France and the rest of Europe.

Balladur seems to have arrived at a "New Realism" over Europe. With the stress of interest rates diminished and GATT concluded, the French could contemplate with more equanimity the disappointing state of the Franco-German couple and the likelihood that the EMU would take longer than originally planned. Likewise, success on GATT indicated that even with limits on what Europe could become in the near future, the EU was far from dead, and French leadership could still mobilize the Union. Moreover, it was rare for Franco-German relations to remain in the doldrums for long—nor did they.

NATO Summit

The NATO summit of January 1994 faced two main issues: to find a modus vivendi between the desire of East European nations to join NATO and the alliance's then reluctance to grant full membership and to develop a framework for NATO's relationship with the European Security and Defense Initiative (ESDI). The first issue was managed through the Partnership for Peace. With respect to the second, French officials seemed convinced that the NATO summit has ushered in a new era of Franco-U.S. cooperation. They were satisfied that the summit had opened the way to developing an effective ESDI. The French were pleased by both the process and outcomes of the recent NATO summit. In terms of process, they attached great importance to the fact that much of the preparatory work of the summit had been accomplished through sustained Franco-U.S. collaboration. With respect to outcomes, they saw the summit as not merely marking U.S. acceptance of the concept of ESDI but as providing through the concept of Combined Joint Task Forces the material means necessary for it to operate. Thus Europe would be able to act effectively in out-of-area conflicts when the United States chose not to intervene.

A negative assessment of developments in the former Soviet Union and fear of Russian expansionism seem to be a major driving force behind France's vocal support for NATO and for a continued U.S. military presence in Europe. The French believe that their vital interests are menaced by a potentially dangerous expansionist Russia—and, in this regard, the United States continues to be the only Western nation that can counteract that threat.

French officials do not believe that there will be significant economic reform in Russia. They expect high inflation rates and economic chaos, which will benefit extremists. They take very seriously the Zhirinovsky phenomenon, if not the man himself. But above all, they believe that a concerted Russian effort to regain de facto control of the near abroad is well under way. If the attempt continues and the Ukrainian situation explodes, the West would have to provide security guarantees for Eastern Europe. There is even interest in the possibility of full NATO membership for the Visegrad Four.

Another reason for increased emphasis on NATO and relations with the United States is limited expectations of what Germany can do in the field of security. Obvious frustration at Germany's inability to play a more active role in security has contributed to a surprisingly warm rapprochement with the UK — facilitated by the UK's willingness to play more of a role within European security institutions and perhaps also by the bad state of relations with the United States.

Bosnia

January 1994 ended with a public polemic between French Foreign Minister Alain Juppé and U.S. Secretary of State Warren Christopher over Bosnia. But by mid-February NATO had taken a military engagement over Bosnia and by the end of the month NATO forces had seen action for the first time in NATO's history. A Franco-U.S. conflict had been transformed into Franco-U.S. cooperation that had changed the nature of Western involvement in former Yugoslavia.

French activism on Bosnia resulted from the determination of Foreign Minister Alain Juppé to focus his attention on Bosnia and obtain a solution as well as the feeling that France was caught in a trap. The policy of providing humanitarian assistance backed by UNPROFOR was no longer viable; UN forces lacked credibility and were being constantly harassed and sometimes killed. On the other hand, withdrawing French troops could lead to an extension of the conflict. The on-again, off-again Geneva peace talks were going nowhere. With Bosnian forces finally gaining some ground against the Bosnian Croats, the government was reluctant to accept a partition that constituted acquiescence in previous Serb victories. The French feared that if the Bosnian Serbs and Croats began a serious counteroffensive, the West might be faced in extremis with the threat of large-scale massacres of the Bosnian Moslems. The French were convinced that the only way to make progress was to obtain U.S. involvement. Their idea was that the United States should pressure the Moslems to negotiate while NATO pressured the Serbs – by opening the Tuzla airport and relieving Srebenica, both deemed security zones by previous UN resolutions.

Warren Christopher's visit to Paris in late January 1994 led not to an understanding between the secretary of state and the French but instead to a polemic: the United States would not pressure the Moslems, the aggrieved party, to negotiate; it would not put in U.S. ground troops before a peace settlement; and it still supported lifting the arms embargo on the Moslems. The French complained that the United States had no plan but was blocking theirs. The State Department accused the French of engaging in a "strange moral calculus" in wanting to pressure the Moslems to accept an unfavorable peace that would require "massive intervention of ground troops by the West, to, in effect, force a settlement upon unwilling partners."[2] Despite this polemic, discussions continued between the United States and France to come up with a joint approach.

On February 5, the bloody attack on the market of Sarajevo changed the situation. The French quickly announced a much grander proposal that involved lifting the siege of Sarajevo and creating a security zone of 30 kilometers around the city. The plan, which would be backed by NATO airpower, encountered a more positive U.S. response. The mortar attack had catalyzed those in the U.S. administration who believed that U.S. policy in Bosnia was eroding NATO's credibility as well as America's reputation and swayed some of those who had been ambivalent. Moreover, the proposal focused on the siege of Sarajevo by the Serbs and required Serb compliance. It put French UNPROFOR forces in jeopardy.

The French proposal was welcomed by a United States in search of a policy. The United States slightly modified it and sold to the NATO allies. Within a matter of days, a NATO ultimatum was delivered that met with significant Serb compliance. Russia, far from opposing NATO action, provided a diplomatic cover for the Serbs. On February 28, NATO forces shot down four Bosnian Serb planes engaged in bombing a munitions factory in Bosnia. A new chapter opened in the Bosnian crisis, although certainly not the last, as did a new chapter in U.S.-French relations. In the words of a senior NATO diplomat quoted by the *New York Times* (February 9, 1994), "What has emerged is Franco-American joint leadership" that was being broadened into overall consensus in NATO.

An Algerian Morass?

The bad news of early 1994 was the increasing probability that Islamic fundamentalists would seize power in Algeria. French analysts believed that the Algerian government was incapable of making the reforms necessary to prevent a fundamentalist victory, but French policy continued to support the government for want of an alternative. Nor did France take well to any U.S. contacts with the Islamic opposition, even on a low level.

French preoccupations with Algeria can hardly be overstated. If a fundamentalist seizure of power were to take place, hundreds of thousands of refugees from the Algerian professional and middle classes would seek admission to France. Unfortunately, they might not be well received by a country suffering from massive unemployment whose public opinion on immigration has been greatly affected by a racist party. National Front (FN) supporters might hardly take the trouble to differentiate between secular Moslems and fundamentalists.

If an Islamic takeover were to occur in Algeria, France would likely receive urgent calls by Tunisia and Morocco to guarantee their security against what might be an interventionist and crusading Algerian fundamentalist regime. A fundamentalist government would probably be hostile to France, because France has done its best to bolster its predecessor. Thus, France might also face the threat of terrorism emanating from Algiers as well as conflicts between Algerians in France. All this raises the possibility that France could become as obsessively trapped in the Algerian situation as it was during the Algerian War, with a corresponding decline of French ability to play an active role elsewhere and a concomitant strain on French resources. These resources have already been strained by France's commitments all over the world, including sub-Saharan Africa, and by French efforts to maintain or even slightly increase military spending at a time when most of its allies are doing the opposite.

4

Domestic Politics:
The Quest for Identity

... And now remains
That we find out the cause of this effect,
Or rather say, the cause of this defect,
For this effect defective comes by cause.

—Hamlet

Tout commence en mystique et finit en politique.

—Péguy

It is impossible to discuss whether France still counts in the European and international arena without considering its domestic politics. A few years ago, a discussion of domestic politics might not have required an entire chapter. It could have been plausibly asserted that partisan politics and international affairs were virtually separate domains and that the institutions of the Fifth Republic and the consensus of the political class guaranteed the stability and consistency of French foreign and European policy. Since the referendum on the Maastricht Treaty, none of this can be merely assumed.

How effective are the political institutions of the Fifth Republic in marshaling French power? Political institutions can contribute to the capacity of a nation to play a strong international role or render such an effort nugatory. Does France now have the domestic political cohesion and will to support its traditional desire for European and international influence? Domestic politics can affect the stability of a regime, divert leaders from critical issues of European construction and the new international order, and distort foreign policy. To what extent is this happening in France?

An Effective Institutional Base

The institutional structure of the Fifth Republic was created by Charles de Gaulle to provide an effective way for France to maximize its influence in foreign and European policy. Like Louis XIV and Napoleon, de Gaulle wanted to create stable political institutions that could support France's claims to great power status in the world. Thus, the strengths of the Fifth Republic's political institutions relate directly to foreign policy. The Constitution centralizes power in the hands of the president of the republic and provides continuity by giving him a seven-year term.

The Constitution of the Fifth Republic embodies the lessons drawn by de Gaulle from the failures of the French political system during his lifetime. The Third Republic was unable to defend French national interest against Adolf Hitler's Germany. De Gaulle, who had failed to convince the army's gerontocrats of the need for an offensive military doctrine in the 1930s found few political leaders willing to support his case. Most of the same political leaders who had failed to listen to his warnings in the 1930s failed to heed his appeal to resist on June 18, 1940. They knuckled under to Hitler and supported the collaborationist Vichy regime under Marshal Philippe Pétain, mistakenly believing that the war was lost. De Gaulle founded Free France, the French resistance movement based in London, to ensure that France would be present in the Allied victory and thus able to retain its place as a great power after the war. At the Liberation, he was determined to replace the Third Republic with a stable political system in which national interest prevailed over party spirit.

Yet de Gaulle's efforts to shape the Constitution of the Fourth Republic were defeated by the very political parties de Gaulle wanted to subjugate. The general watched the Fourth Republic go the way of the Third in the face of the Indochina and Algerian conflicts. Once again, a weak and unstable political system was not able to cope with external dangers. When de Gaulle returned to power in 1958, he imposed the kind of constitution he wanted. The Fifth Republic constitution combines elements of a presidential and parliamentary regime but the political practice of the de Gaulle period even more than the letter of the constitution made the Fifth Republic into a presidential republic. The lack of serious parliamentary control; the cohesion, homogeneity, and effectiveness of the French bureaucracy; and the fact that France is essentially a unitary rather than federal state all enable the president to effectively project French power and influence abroad while maintaining peace and economic growth at home.[1]

French political history since the revolution has been characterized by instability, punctuated by revolutionary shifts from one form of government to another. No previous regime had succeeded in both obtaining near common consent for its legitimacy and effectively defending French national interest over an extended period. At its inception, the Constitution of the Fifth Republic was not accepted by much of the Fourth Republic's political elite, including François Mitterrand. But with the socialist victory of 1981 and Mitterrand's entry into the Elysée, opposition to the constitution disappeared. Of the politicians who played an active role in the Fourth Republic, there is virtually no one left but Mitterrand. The composition of the French political class has radically changed. There is little nostalgia for the Fourth Republic.

There are, however, two potential weaknesses in the

Fifth Republic's constitution – the problem of "cohabitation" and the atrophy of Parliament. Cohabitation occurs when the president of the republic is from one side of the political spectrum and the parliamentary majority and thus the government from the other. French leaders were haunted by the fear of cohabitation until it finally occurred in 1986. Because of the long tradition of adversarial politics in France, it was hard to imagine how the minimal necessary cooperation to keep government functioning would be obtained. In addition, there were few precedents for such a situation, which does not occur in a parliamentary regime. One precedent – the cohabitation between Louis Napoleon and the National Assembly of the Second Republic – ended unhappily with a coup d'état in 1851.[2]

On the two occasions cohabitation has occurred in the Fifth Republic (from 1986 to 1988 and from April 1993 to the present), the declining popularity of the president and governing party led to a change in parliamentary majority five years into the presidential term. Although in both cases cohabitation coincided with preparations for presidential elections, it was not inherently destabilizing. The first time, there were considerable tensions between President Mitterrand and Prime Minister Jacques Chirac, both contenders in the 1988 presidential elections, especially over demarcating their respective roles in foreign policy. Yet the public wanted government by the center in a country lacking a strong center party and found cohabitation to its liking.

That cohabitation succeeded at all testified to the decline of ideology in French politics and accelerated the trend toward pragmatism. Despite fire-eating words in 1992–1993 by some conservative politicians about forcing Mitterrand out, so far the second period of cohabitation has proceeded far more smoothly than the first. Indeed Prime Minister Edouard Balladur has more in common with the president and probably enjoys better relations with him than with prominent leaders of his own party. The situation could, of course, change with the onset of presidential elections. Cohabitation in France might begin to occur as frequently as when U.S. presidents face opposition control of one or both houses of Congress – with no greater consequences for political stability and good government.

The second problem of the Fifth Republic is that the growth of presidential power and the state has corresponded with the atrophy of Parliament. In the early 1990s, it was commonplace that the only elected officials who mattered were the president of the republic and the mayors. The constitution as shaped by three decades of practice had weakened the powers of prime minister, government, and Parliament during periods when the president's supporters held a majority in the assembly – to the point that not only opposition but majority deputies were unhappy. The long-standing problem of overcentralization of power in Paris remains despite the creation of regions and the weakening of the prefects. But it is hard to see how these problems can be remedied by the proposals for constitutional reform that have been brought up only to be adjourned, nor is a return to the Fourth Republic or the adoption of U.S. institutions likely. Indeed, the Fourth Republic constitutes a kind of bogeyman that can be raised to oppose any effort to increase the role of Parliament.

The length of the presidential term and the possibility of reelection reinforces the possibility that a president's tenure will outlast his welcome. De Gaulle's near absolute powers were barely a match for the peculiar revolt of May 1968 – a student uprising that led to a general strike and national paralysis, briefly threatening the very survival of the regime. Political actors and analysts alike are haunted by the fear it could happen again. May 1968 was a complete surprise.[3] There is some reason to think that without the Right's electoral success in 1993, Mitterrand might have suffered a similar fate. By weakening all intermediary institutions between president and public, the Fifth Republic creates a void in which popular discontent cannot be channeled. Near absolute political power can prove brittle. That is the Achilles' heel of a system that at least so far has provided the president with an excellent means of developing and implementing long-term foreign and European policy with minimal interference.

The Content of French Politics

Does France have the political cohesion to support a significant European and international role? To answer this question requires addressing the nature of contemporary French politics and facing, at the outset, an apparent paradox: in the last decade, French politics has seemed on a roller coaster. The socialists who came to power in 1981 were defeated in the parliamentary elections of 1986. Mitterrand was reelected in 1988 and dissolved the National Assembly. The socialists then returned to government, only to suffer crushing defeat in 1993. Still, there has been remarkable stability in the policies followed by governments of the Left and Right. Two factors explain the paradox: in the last decade the political class has developed consensus on major policy issues, and the economic policies followed by governments for a decade and a half have been unsuccessful in alleviating unemployment, which is at the root of France's pervasive malaise.

In the fall of 1989, *Le Point* editor Claude Imbert described in a *Foreign Affairs* article ("The End of French Exceptionalism") the tardy arrival in France of what Daniel Bell had termed the "end of ideology" in the 1960s. In 1981 no one could have anticipated the "end of ideology" in France. The election of 1981 had been fought with almost as much excitement as the Popular Front election of 1936 and had polarized France nearly as much.[4] The French Socialist Party (PS) abjured the label of social-democrat and vowed to "change life" and create an alternative to capitalism. The passionate commitment of the socialists to change had been nurtured by decades of exclusion from political power. Yet Mitterrand's proposed foreign and defense policy differed only in nuance from his predecessor's, and his domestic programs, proposed while he enjoyed an absolute socialist majority in the National Assembly, did not prove revolutionary, innovative, or effective. Far from bringing France out of recession, the policies deepened it. Within three years, Mitterrand was forced to return to centrist economic policies.

In 1986, the Right, animated by an enthusiasm for laissez-faire economics that was alien to its heritage, vowed to march France off in the direction of privatization and free market economics. Public opinion and the uneasiness of its own parliamentarians prevented the Chirac government of 1986–1988 from straying very far. When Mitterrand was reelected in 1988 and the socialists returned to the government, the ambition of the Rocard government was to pursue consensus economic policies.[5]

At the same time, Mitterrand had succeeded in weakening the power of the French Communist Party, whose great electoral and ideological strength had helped keep the socialists left and French politics ideological.[6] By the 1980s, the French Communist Party (PCF) under Georges Marchais had become fossilized and irrelevant, even before its humiliation following the collapse of the USSR. The PCF remains a political fact, albeit diminished, but no longer much of a force. French politics, once the forum of intense ideological debate, became largely the struggle between ins and outs who, except at the extremes, differed little in program and perhaps only slightly more in temperament. On the face of it, the end of French exceptionalism seems to mark the triumph of pragmatism and the acceptance of a more American style of politics. Unfortunately, it also presents two serious problems. First, it is difficult to maintain a party system based on Left-Right differences when Left and Right no longer differ much. Second, centrist economic policies did not alleviate unemployment. On the contrary, unemployment has remained stagnant or has risen during the last 15 years.

Since the French Revolution, the French party system has been based on Left-Right differences that initially correlated to attitudes toward religion and political ideology but by the twentieth century were more tied to class and socioeconomic issues. These issues are no longer salient. A multiparty political system whose main parties differ on men but not measures runs the risk of alienating the general public — *especially during an extended period of recession.* For at least the last decade (and arguably much longer), *French politics has been driven by discontent about the economy — and in particular unemployment.* Because no government has succeeded in solving the problem, each election has produced an alternation of power — but the same policies have continued.

The French Malaise

What happens when French voters lose faith in the ability of democratic parties to solve basic economic problems? Popular anxiety has led to the development of a pervasive malaise based on fears about the economy but drawing on other areas of anxiety, particularly immigration. The malaise has resulted in higher abstention rates during elections and the rise and persistence of nontraditional and antisystem parties. Ideology, which exited through the front door, returns in different guise through the back door.

France has been one of the most statist economies in Europe. If the UK and the United States are models of free market economies, France is a model of a planned economy. The inability of the state to solve problems leads to questions about its viability, which in turn evokes a fundamental ambivalence in the French mentality. France has a long tradition of both wanting to be governed and resenting strong authority. For the last 200 years, French politics has attempted to reconcile these two seemingly incompatible desires. But what the French resent most is when relatively autocratic rule proves ineffective. Much of the pervasive malaise of the early 1990s stems from the perception that the state could no longer defend the national interest and the president himself had failed to master the situation.

On the whole, unemployment in France has continued to increase since the Giscard presidency. This rise has been punctuated not by periods of significant decline in unemployment but only by periods of stagnation. Since 1991, unemployment has risen from 9 percent to 12 percent and continues to rise. In France as well as in the United States, unemployment is generally the major concern of the public; dealing with it has been a main promise of the political parties in every national campaign. It is not surprising that unemployment constitutes the basis for a deep malaise and that its persistence is blamed on the political parties, the political system, and finally on the state itself. Thus unemployment ceases to be just a short-term problem of the French economy and raises questions about the vulnerability of the French economy, as the state moves away from *dirigisme* and as more economic policies are set by Brussels (and Frankfurt).

Another cause of the malaise is immigration, which is tied to levels of unemployment and fears of unemployment. In the 1990 SOFRES polls, immigration was the second preoccupation of the French, exceeded only by unemployment; 68 percent believed there were too many immigrants in France. But when the questions were raised about specific social groups, the only group to which this judgment applied was Arabs. Ironically, 69 percent of those questioned had not experienced any family or personal problems with regard to immigrants.[7] Fear and hostility are specifically directed at Arab immigrants who are perceived as unwilling or incapable of being assimilated rather than just as constituting an economic threat.

A succession of political scandals has deepened the malaise. Historically, antiparliamentary movements have thrived on scandals, many of which (Panama, Stavisky, et cetera) involved the connection between illicit money and politicians.[8] A succession of "affaires" came to light during the second Mitterrand term. Many involved illicit means used by political parties (rather than individuals) to finance their operations, a common problem in a country that unlike Germany has not clearly defined a system for party financing. Although each scandal was seized upon by one or several parties to discredit its enemies, the parties in general and the political system as a whole were all tarnished. The socialists, as the governing party and apparently the largest beneficiary, were the great losers in electoral terms. They also were deeply damaged by a different kind of scandal, the contamination of French blood transfusion supplies by the AIDS virus and the failure of officials to inform patients receiving transfusions. The question of responsibility—whether it extended to the ministerial level or even implicated then Prime Minister Laurent Fabius—also damaged the PS.

At a time when high unemployment catalyzed fears about immigration and the major political parties had become sober preachers of the same dismal science, it is not surprising that the National Front enjoyed some success.[9] Begun as a right-wing protest movement, the FN has proven durable and robust. The political survival of its leader Jean-Marie Le Pen not only reflects persistent discontent in France but contributes to even greater malaise by corrupting the political and moral atmosphere. The fact that France has never fully come to terms with the Vichy experience facilitates his efforts.

There is nothing unusual about the National Front except its success. It resembles its right-wing extremist forebears, like the Poujadist movement of the 1950s, in its antipathy for the Left, the party system, its attacks on corruption, demands for authoritarian leadership, hatred of foreigners (especially Arabs), antisemitism, and self-proclaimed concern for the "forgotten man." The rise of the National Front was initially aided by high unemployment and the 1981 victory of the socialists. As was the case in the 1930s, the Left in power mobilizes the far Right. The FN drew disenchanted protest votes from the Right as well as from former communists. Above all, Le Pen used the immigration issue to create a mass populist movement. What differentiates the FN from previous movements is its durability—it has survived conservative electoral victories and dug roots.

The political system is not directly threatened by Le Pen or the National Front's coming to power. Nor has the FN succeeded in obtaining more than minimal representation in the National Assembly in the last two elections. Its main impact is the pressure it exerts on the traditional Right. In the early 1990s, the traditional Right became so anxious to win back the voters it had lost to Le Pen that its leaders began to imitate his rhetoric. Jacques Chirac empathized with Frenchmen forced to suffer the body odor of immigrants, and Valéry Giscard d'Estaing referred to an immigrant "invasion," asking that citizenship be accorded exclusively on the "right of blood" rather than the "right of soil." Even socialist prime minister Edith Cresson resurrected the old rightist threat to charter planes to send back illegal immigrants. The political game has thus helped to legitimize Le Pen's rhetoric and agenda, debasing politics and undermining democratic institutions. (The Right would claim that it had no other way of stemming Le Pen's efforts to take over its constituencies.) In October 1991, one out of three Frenchmen shared Le Pen's ideas as opposed to 18 percent in September 1990. The figure fell to 19 percent in January 1994 (*Le Monde*, February 4, 1994). The debate over Maastricht allowed the FN to tie its fears about loss of French identity to anxieties about European integration.

The National Front was not the only beneficiary of the malaise. The ecologist parties gained votes at the expense of the socialists, although like the National Front they could not convert that support into seats in the National Assembly in the 1993 elections. There has also been a rising tide of electoral abstentionism.

The other side of the French malaise was a loss of faith in the president and his government. Mitterrand's reelection in 1988 was not a ringing endorsement; the elections of 1988 were less a testimonial to Mitterrand's record or the program of the Socialist Party than a repudiation of his opponents on the Right, including the incumbent prime minister Chirac. François Mitterrand's apparent loss of flair in running French foreign policy during his second term catalyzed domestic discontent. Doubts about Mitterrand's handling of foreign policy crystallized after he initially seemed to accept the August 1991 Soviet coup as a fait accompli and failed to express support for Gorbachev, Boris Yeltsin, or the constitutional authorities. The parallel of his failure to react well and effectively was soon drawn with his halting response to German unification. These faux pas were attributed to a variety of causes, including reluctance to accept changes in the status quo, a slowness in grasping new realities, the side effects of prostate cancer, and a decline in the president's mental acuteness. In any case, the result was at least momentary questioning of Mitterrand's competence in the core area of his presidential authority – foreign policy – an area where he had always scored high marks and continued to record successes.

After his reelection, Mitterrand appointed his old rival Michel Rocard as prime minister but emasculated his powers in denying him the chance to try to break the mold of French politics by creating a genuine coalition government with the center. Commentators agreed that France was emmeshed in a policy of drift (la dérive) before the outbreak of the Gulf War. The war temporarily improved Mitterrand's popularity, but as was the case with U.S. President George Bush, its benefits were ephemeral. Rocard was dismissed just after the Gulf War, when Mitterrand's popularity had begun to ebb and unemployment began to rise. His successor Edith Cresson proved an enormous political liability. Mitterrand awaited the expected PS debacle in the regional/cantonal elections to oust Cresson, so as not to implicate her successor in the defeat. Mitterrand then chose his faithful supporter Pierre Bérégevoy, one of the handful of socialist leaders who had been a worker and who generally maintained high marks for his probity as prime minister.

Bérégevoy, despite his personal reputation, was unable to turn the political situation around. His government zealously defended the franc, but failed to reduce unemployment, while the European economy suffered under high German interest rates. The succession of scandals continued, and even Bérégevoy was attacked for having accepted an interest-free loan from a businessman accused of insider trading (a charge that seems to have been a major impetus in driving Bérégevoy to suicide after the socialists lost the elections of 1993).

Mitterrand's unpopularity proved an incubus that could not be exorcised. The threat of electoral catastrophe accentuated tensions between factions within the Socialist Party and tensions between the party and Mitterrand himself. For some socialists, Mitterrand constituted an obstacle to the survival of the party. And as time went on, Mitterrand may well have begun to think how he personally could survive the PS's defeat. The same man who had patiently rebuilt the Socialist Party in the 1970s now had brought it full circle to a rout that many believed was fatal (whence the bitter joke that Mitterrand loved the Socialist Party so much that he wanted to leave it the way he had found it in 1971). With too many leaders and thus no leadership, the defeatist socialists went into the election with little hope of winning and less desire to campaign. Unable to mobilize their own voters, they failed to get the support of either communists or ecologists. Their defeat was inevitable, their rout self-inflicted. But the collapse of the socialists was in no way the equivalent of a mandate for the Right.

Mitterrand's decision to hold a referendum on Maastricht took place during the period when he was striving desperately to find a way to block the electoral victory of the Right in the legislative elections – and to save himself from the unpleasant prospect of cohabitation. The referendum did no such thing. Instead, it made the Treaty of Maastricht the lightning rod for popular anxiety, thereby threatening a kind of elite politics in which the political class excluded the public from involvement in issues critical to the French national interest.

Maastricht and French Politics

The formulation of Maastricht inspired no real debate on Europe by Parliament and the nation and provoked little awareness that great choices were being made. There were more divisions within than between parties. Although European integration per se was not a matter of deep concern to Frenchmen, if grafted onto the widespread fears of immigration and the sense of loss of national identity, it could become part of a potent complex of fears manipulated by the extreme Right. A signal of how sensitive the question of French identity had become was the earlier debate over a statute to grant Corsica autonomy. The first article of that statute, which recognizes the Corsicans as a "composite part of the French people" was the subject of a long parliamentary debate, in which opposition leaders denied its compatibility with the concept of a French people one and indivisible, a position ultimately endorsed by the Constitutional Council, which declared it unconstitutional. But the danger of a significant rift in France over the Maastricht Treaty was by no means inevitable. Ironically, it was François Mitterrand himself who helped bring it about. The French government had felt a sense of urgency about drafting and signing the treaty, but it had no similar sense of urgency about ratification, in France or elsewhere.

As a result of an April 1992 decision by the Constitutional Council that the treaty required prior amendment of the constitution because of three areas of incompatibility between existing constitutional texts and the treaty, a two-stage process of first amending the constitution and then ratifying the treaty had to be used. Each step could be accomplished either through a purely parliamentary procedure, requiring an absolute majority in both the National

Assembly and Senate followed by a three-fifths majority in a joint session of Parliament (known as a Congress). There was an overwhelming majority in support of the treaty. On May 13, 1992, the National Assembly voted 398 to 77 to approve the requisite constitutional changes, with almost all socialists and centrists voting in favor. The members of the RPR (Rally for the Republic) generally abstained; 31 voted against. RPR attempts to place restrictive amendments failed. The vote and the debate that preceded it demonstrated the potential of this issue for dividing the UDF (Union for French Democracy) from the RPR and also for promoting internal divisions within the RPR.

After the defeat of the Danish referendum, Mitterrand's quick decision to call for a popular referendum to ratify the treaty occurred before the Senate had yet considered the constitutional amendment passed by the assembly. This decision reflected the president's desire to restore legitimacy and momentum to the European project by demonstrating the strength of French support. But it also afforded ample opportunities for the president to play on divisions in the Right before the legislative elections. The president hoped to regain popularity by supporting what the polls indicated to be a very popular treaty.

At first Mitterrand's decision to hold a referendum seemed politically astute. Most of the political class closed ranks in support of the treaty. Pro-Maastricht personalities from the government and opposition held joint meetings throughout the country to the consternation of the RPR, which threatened the UDF with dire if unnamed consequences if it continued to participate. But the RPR, itself profoundly divided and virtually paralyzed on the issue of Maastricht, was in no position to reproach its UDF allies. The two principal opponents of Maastricht, Charles Pasqua and Philippe Séguin, were both from the RPR, whereas RPR secretary-general Alain Juppé was a strong proponent. So was Edouard Balladur, already a serious candidate to be the next prime minister. Jacques Chirac, alleged to be personally in favor of the treaty, did not want to estrange the extreme Right, which he hoped to win back from the FN and the anti-Europeans within his party. He also could not afford to alienate the center and the UDF. He delayed taking a position until July 5, deciding that the RPR would not take a stand on the referendum but that he personally would vote in favor. Giscard d'Estaing, his main conservative rival for the presidency, hoped to transmute his zeal for the European cause into political gold for the presidential elections – and in the short term to obtain for the UDF a majority in the new conservative majority expected to emerge from the 1993 legislative elections.

The referendum on the Treaty of Maastricht of September 20, 1992, was the first time the French public voted directly on the issue of France's future in Europe. The narrow margin of victory for the affirmative position constituted a clear warning of the fragility of the political elite's position; a change in 1 percent of the vote could have gravely damaged decades of effort to create a new European structure, an effort largely inspired by France.

Political scientists Olivier Duhamel and Gérard Grunberg argue that the referendum indicated five basic sociological dichotomies. In general, support for the treaty came more from those who were well-educated and well-off than from those who were not, from those who were politically more in the center than those on the extremes, from those whose values were more permissive than repressive, from populations more urban than rural, and from those more socialist-christian than nationalist-laicist.[10] But given the extent of support by the political, economic, and intellectual/cultural elite, it is hard not to conclude that almost half of the French population rejected its leadership. Mitterrand, instead of winning a plebiscite, received a slap in the face that further weakened his presidency and demoralized his party. The real winners were politicians like Philippe Séguin, who by taking the "unpopular" cause gained a notoriety that propelled them into public prominence and made anti-European feelings and economic nationalism respectable.

The referendum campaign revealed the existence of a

"party of movement" that supports the progressive Euro-
peanization and modernization of France and a "party of
reaction" that opposes it. But these virtual "parties" did
not correspond to existing political formations. The new
configurations were clearly visible at the time of the referendum, which produced groupings of leaders across existing party lines. In practice, the elites that voted "yes" on
the referendum, regardless of political affiliation, are members of the "party of movement" that has governed France
since Giscard's presidency. They engineered the transformation of France without the voting public's having been
explicitly consulted.

Obviously, the vote was not only a vote about Europe
but also an expression of discontent about the political
elite and in particular the president. The question is, does
this referendum mark a short-lived surfacing of public irritation based on circumstantial factors or a vote of no-
confidence in the elite and its policies? Does the opposition
to Maastricht of Philippe Séguin and others signify the
beginning of a breakdown of elite consensus or a minor
rebellion? The answers to these questions could determine
whether France possesses the cohesion and will to exercise
European and international influence. But the decisive fac-
tor could be the government's success in dealing with unemployment and the economy.

The Balladur Government

The Balladur government came to power in the aftermath
of the Right's landslide (in seats, if not in votes) in the April
1993 elections but also in the aftermath of the Maastricht
referendum. It constitutes a veritable "Ministry of All the
Talents" of a Right that has been out of office for all but 2
of the last 13 years. It includes not only established political figures but many up and coming younger ministers
like Alain Juppé at the Ministry of Foreign Affairs and
Edmond Alphandéry at the Ministry of the Economy. Much

of the government's popularity derives from the reassuring and courtly style of Prime Minister Balladur. Because of the lack of fundamental policy difference between Mitterrand and Balladur in the area of international and European affairs and the absence of personal animus, cohabitation began well. The suicide of Bérégevoy produced a reaction that may also have served to shield members of the new government from the kind of personal attacks suffered by the old.

Although such veterans of the anti-Maastricht campaign as Charles Pasqua and François Fillon received domestic portfolios (Philippe Séguin became president of the National Assembly), the government is dominated by figures of the party of movement. Government policy generally represents continuity with the previous administration. The most significant difference seems to be a great deal of tough talk by Minister of Interior Charles Pasqua on law and order and immigration, including statements that France would henceforth be a country of zero immigration (later modified to "zero illegal immigration" – hardly the same thing). The purpose of Pasqua's grandstanding is largely to win back rightist voters who have flirted with the National Front. But the government has also passed laws restricting immigration, some of which were rejected by the Constitutional Council for violating constitutional provisions. The government responded by revising the constitution. In some ways, the Balladur government runs the risk of being the victim of its own success. Its image of competence and popularity arouse public expectations for immediate success – above all in economic issues. Its immense parliamentary majority (similar to but much bigger than that of the PS in 1981) affords no alibi for failure. Likewise, the president, having little influence over domestic legislation, cannot be turned into a scapegoat for failure. The weakness of the opposition parties within Parliament makes it difficult to maintain discipline in the assembly.

The unity of the government is menaced for reasons of both politics and policy. In terms of politics, the major problem has seemed to be that coalition discipline would break down rapidly as presidential elections approached. Balladur was not originally expected to be a presidential candidate. Even under the unlikely circumstances of a single candidate of the RPR and UDF on the first ballot, there would have to be a "primary" to choose that candidate, with the event preceded by intense partisan politics and polemic boding ill for governmental solidarity. It seemed likely that political ambitions would prove too strong for the principles of conservative unity (more honored in the breach than in the observance), that both Chirac and Giscard would insist on running, and that some younger conservative politicians might also run (as well as Le Pen).

Since that time, Balladur's continuing popularity has transformed the situation. His masterful handling of the GATT turned into a major foreign and domestic triumph. Balladur appears the obvious candidate of the Right, eclipsing his former political master and "friend of 30 years" Jacques Chirac. But it is unlikely that Chirac will give up easily. Unless polls indicate that he cannot defeat Rocard, it is hard to see how Chirac could fail to get the nomination of the RPR. Conventional wisdom in early 1994 held that Balladur would not be a candidate against Chirac if Chirac had the formal backing of the RPR, but that is not obvious. As for Rocard and the socialists, their only hope is internecine conflict on the Right. Balladur's credibility, however, has been affected by his willingness to appease movements of social protest by backing down from government positions.

In the European elections, the combined UDF/RPR list scored a poor 25.5 percent and the PS a miserable 14.5. A pro-Maastricht slate under Bernard Tapie (who was encouraged in this enterprise by Mitterrand himself) received 12 percent (much of it presumably siphoned off from the PS vote), and an anti-Maastricht slate led by UDF dissident Philippe de Villiers obtained 12 percent as well. The socialist defeat, followed by infighting that led to the departure of Michel Rocard as party leader, further undermines PS prospects in the presidential elections. The results on the

Right also weaken the chances for a common UDF/RPR candidate on the first ballot of the presidential elections.

In terms of policy, the government is divided between the party of movement and the party of reaction, with Balladur generally on the side of the first but with some partiality toward national economic policy and European protectionism linking him to the latter. The Balladur government is faced with rising unemployment. Unfortunately, no government action is likely to produce quick results. And so long as France operates within the framework of the strong franc and the EMS, it is hard to see what kind of unilateral action it can take. To break with that framework runs the risk of vitiating monetary union and European cohesion, the fruits of decades of Franco-German cooperation. The Balladur government would not do this for policy reasons; moreover, for it to take any measures in this direction would play into the hands of political opponents like Séguin. It is even less likely to do so now that German interest rates have been cut. The government thus finds itself somewhat paralyzed on the very issue that most affects its political survival. That paralysis is compounded by Balladur's fear of another May 1968. To avoid such a crisis, Balladur has tended to back down when programs involving economic restructuring or modernization result in protest by significant interest groups (Air France employees, farmers, fishermen).

All of this foreshadows political volatility. Initially, this has manifested itself in conflict within the conservative majority. Philippe Séguin's speech of June 16, 1993, calling for "a complete reversal of values and fundamental choices," constitutes not only the manifesto of the party of reaction but also of the opposition to the Balladur government from within its own majority. But Séguin is only the John the Baptist of the "autre politique." The wild card is whether a major politician, specifically Jacques Chirac, will break ranks with the political class consensus and take up Séguin's banner. Chirac might be tempted to do so if economic conditions decline drastically and he saw it as the only way of preventing Balladur from becoming the consensus candidate of the Right. Infighting on the Right threatens the future of the Balladur government far more than do the weakened parties of the opposition. Unlike Michel Rocard, Chirac could conceivably also threaten the continuity of French policy. The combination of policy and politics could conceivably lead to a debate over economic and monetary policy that could split the political elite and thereby make foreign and European policy a subject of mass politics – with potentially adverse consequences for France's influence in Europe.

5

Franco-U.S. Relations

The pressure of immediate crises, foreign and domestic, should not obfuscate the fact that one of the Clinton administration's inescapable foreign policy challenges is to work out a new security relationship with Europe based on greater partnership and equality. Indeed, the ability to build such a new partnership may determine whether Europe and the United States can work together to parry threats and defuse crises likely to occur in Eastern Europe and the former Soviet Union, but the exact nature or gravity of which cannot be predicted.

Establishing a new relationship with Europe in turn requires recognizing the need to deal effectively with France. France, far more than Germany or the UK, will be the political leader of Europe for at least the rest of the decade. If the United States could achieve reconciliation with its archenemy, the former Soviet Union, should it not be able to attain cooperation with its oldest ally?

At the center of U.S.-French relations since World War I – and at the heart of Franco-U.S. conflicts – have been issues relating to security. Likewise, the future of the relationship depends on security cooperation. Only by understanding the causes for conflict during the cold war is it possible to move ahead to greater cooperation after the cold war.

The key to understanding French security policy is to understand French perceptions of their national interest. The degree to which the United States and France can cooperate depends on the extent to which their interests converge — and the way both perceive that convergence. It also means improving the culture of U.S.-French relations, because a history of mutual dislike among much of the elite and general public is not without its effect on relations between the two states. At the risk of oversimplifying, it can be argued that U.S.-French relations in the postwar period have gone through two phases and may now be entering a third.

Cold War

With the inception of the cold war, the United States had one major goal — to contain Soviet communism and its allies. For Europe, this policy of containment depended on U.S. nuclear power and a multilateral political-military alliance under U.S. leadership — NATO. Germany's role in World War II became a matter of academic interest for the United States. The U.S. concern was that West German resources — economic, political, and military — be effectively harnessed to the cold war effort.

France's view was more complex. Obviously, France was concerned about the Soviet threat and reassured by the U.S. presence in Europe as well as the nuclear umbrella. At the same time, France needed the military wherewithal to retain its own national independence and world power status (ultimately this required a French nuclear capacity). For some time, France acted as if it had to preserve its colonial empire to retain great power status, but discovered paradoxically that only by abandoning its empire could it retain its status. France also wanted Europe to have maximum autonomy from U.S. domination. Finally, the German question retained high priority. After the war, France returned to the same theses it had advocated in 1918–1919, that the German problem could only be resolved by some combination of dismemberment and repression. The Schuman Plan of 1950 constituted a far more productive approach—the solution lay in including Germany in, and mooring it to, multilateral European institutions. Resolving the German problem thus led to the creation of a European entity, beginning with the Coal and Steel Community.

All the above ideas found expression during the Fourth Republic. But the political weakness and fragmentation of the republic and the problem of colonial wars vitiated its ability to execute them. Under Charles de Gaulle and the Fifth Republic, France was able to implement them, but de Gaulle's own perspective increasingly tended to emphasize the anti-U.S. dimension. France's decision to leave NATO's integrated military command was a major consequence.

What limited French pretensions to national independence or European solidarity and what discouraged other NATO members from choosing Paris over Washington was the continuing reality of the Soviet threat and the need for the U.S. nuclear umbrella. The gap between France and the United States was greater in rhetoric than in practice. In fact, a perceived increase in the Soviet threat accelerated a de facto French rapprochement with NATO and the United States during the Mitterrand presidency.

After the Cold War

With the end of the cold war, the breakdown of the Soviet Union, and the unification of Germany, the threat of the Soviet Union seemed to have ended. French concerns shifted back to the German question. To moor Germany firmly to Europe in economic, monetary, and security terms, France worked for a Maastricht Treaty that aimed at "the eventual framing of a common defense policy, that might in time lead to a common defense." Although there were echoes of de Gaulle's "European Europe" in this phrase, what inspired the French was less enthusiasm for an independent Europe (although there were archaeo-Gaullists ensconced in the administration who thought this way) than fear that the end of the cold war might result in a loss of U.S. interest in Europe. It was necessary to create a European security and defense structure including Germany lest U.S. withdrawal and the end of NATO compel Germany to seek its own national defense.

The positive side was the hope that Europe could become an effective international player. A nation-state the size of France was too small to act effectively; France wanted Europe to be a France writ large. That required a common foreign and security policy, the military instruments necessary to project force, and the willingness to use them. France's ambitions at Maastricht, however, as well as the creation of the Eurocorps, were seen by the United States as efforts to disrupt NATO and consequently met strong opposition from the Bush administration.

Bush Administration Policy

In 1991, many officials in the Bush administration feared that a strong European Community would threaten U.S. economic interests in Europe and marginalize NATO through the creation of a European security system. The Uruguay round of GATT and the future of the WEU became the symbols of U.S. concern; France, the U.S. nemesis, was seen as masterminding an anti-American campaign. U.S. relations with France were in a particularly parlous state after the announcement of the Franco-German corps in the spring of 1991, given U.S. concerns that Franco-German attempts to form a European army corps would undermine NATO. With the exception of a brief tryst during the Gulf War, relations deteriorated throughout the Bush administration.

The attitude toward France of most top U.S. officials, long a mixture of irritation and animosity, stems from resentment that has lived on in the bureaucracy since squabbles with de Gaulle over the U.S. role in Europe in the 1960s. One of the goals of the Bush administration seemed to be to emancipate Europe from French influence. But if France is as marginal as some U.S. policymakers claimed, why were these efforts unsuccessful?

Key figures in the Bush administration falsely believed that they could and should use Britain and Germany to counter French influence. Britain is certainly the European state culturally closest to the United States, but its inability to decide on its own role in the European Community and its diminishing economic weight weaken London's ability to steer the EC. The UK does not want to lead Europe, indeed cannot because it is too weak; its influence is limited because it is not sure that it is European and Europeans mistrust British intentions. Continued talk on the U.S. part about "special relationships" only serves to encourage British wishful thinking that there is an alternative to committing to Europe. It also substantiates European fears that the United States wants to subvert a closer European Community.

After unification in 1990, Germany became the Bush White House's preferred "partner in leadership" (there were second thoughts when Bonn asserted itself over Croatia). But the United States suffers many illusions on this subject, including a belief that Germany can assert decisive leadership in Europe and that Germany shares U.S. political and security vision. The United States fails to understand that Germany has difficulty dealing with its own domestic problems and has learned the lessons of World War II in such a fashion that it is unsure it wants to exercise political leadership in Europe. Many in Germany would prefer to eschew a military role.

Lacking a sense of history, some U.S. policymakers

have not recognized that an effort by Germany to claim political and military leadership would soon lead to the creation of an anti-German coalition in Europe. They do not understand that the postwar peace of Europe reposes on a Franco-German partnership. In the belief that France exercises some kind of Dr. Mabuse-like power over the good Germans, they sometimes think about trying to break that partnership. They fail to see that if the Franco-German tie were broken, the basis for the stability of Western Europe and the EU would be undermined. As Christoph Bertram, a noted pro-U.S. German journalist, wrote in 1992:

> It would be extremely shortsighted for the United States to appeal to U.S.-German bilateralism at the expense of Germany's European role. If Germany were to respond accordingly, this would put the cohesion already achieved within the Community at risk. Were Germany to decline the offer, this would be interpreted, without much justification, as an anti-American move. France under Charles de Gaulle and many of his successors made the fundamental mistake of asking Germany to choose between Paris and Washington, a choice the Germans wisely refused to make. But if the United States were now to ask Germany to choose between Europe and America, Germany would in all probability not pick America.[1]

Franco-German squabbles have never been an asset to U.S. foreign policy, as twentieth-century history testifies.

Two Visions of Security and a Triangular Debate

During the Bush administration, there was a curious debate over European security with two theses and three major players.[2] In reality, there were only two genuine scenarios for Atlantic relations. The traditional Anglo-U.S. view attempted to perpetuate as much as possible the cold war

institutional status quo. Its assumption was that a re-
formed NATO (with decreased U.S. military expense and
presence and with a more political mission) would ensure
U.S. influence and leadership in Europe. The problem with
this position was that it tended to regard institutional
change as a threat to U.S. leadership and failed to define a
role for NATO in the absence of the Soviet Union.

The second scenario for the Atlantic future was
France's. Since 1950, Paris and Bonn have answered the
German question by anchoring Germany and its industrial—hence war-making potential—in multilateral European institutions. The European Coal and Steel Community (forerunner of the EC) was born in 1950 as an
instrument of Franco-German reconciliation but also of
mutually acceptable control. With each step in the process
of EC integration, from Rome in 1957 to Maastricht in
1991, the French have systematically countered any possibility of German unilateralism by attaching Germany ever
more firmly to an increasingly integrated Europe. In the
process, and especially since the Berlin Wall opened
in 1989, the French have decided that the only way they
can continue to play a leadership role in Europe—and
that Europe can play a global role—is by sacrificing a
measure of national independence on the altar of European
integration.

The French vision of a European Union—as already
noted—was France writ large, with a common foreign and
security policy and capacity for defense. It was based on
the belief that these are logically entailed by the development of the European Community. Another rationale (but
secondary, according to the French) was the possibility
that U.S. forces might eventually withdraw from Europe,
making the creation of a European security and defense
structure all the more important. France neither wanted to
have to react overnight to such a withdrawal, nor did it
want Germany to be tempted to seek security indepen-
dently. French efforts were aimed at laying the foundations of such a European Union, not excluding the United

States, although some hard-line archaeo-Gaullists bur-
rowed in the administration may indulge in such a fantasy.

The third party to the debate between the United
States and France was Germany, which sought a synthesis
of, or at least peaceful coexistence with, the opposing theses of the United States and France. Several consequences,
mostly unintended and certainly unexamined, flowed from
this triangular debate:

• The British became irrelevant. As a result of mirror-
ing or even exaggerating the U.S. position, the British were
taken for granted by the Americans and were seen all too
often as outsiders to Europe by the French and Germans.
• In the absence of serious direct U.S.-French dialogue, Germany functioned as an intermediary between
France and the United States.
• The debate unfolded in such a way that neither the
United States nor France *needed* to express the inherent
ambiguity of its respective position. Because the task of
reconciliation was left to the Germans, there was no reason
to weaken one's bargaining position; no real direct negotiations were taking place anyway. This situation played
into the hands of U.S. Francophobes and French archaeo-
Gaullists.
• Germany appeared schizophrenic. Because U.S. and
French positions were so far apart, Germany threw its
weight behind *both* U.S. efforts at increasing the role of
NATO (like the creation of the NACC) *and* French efforts
at strengthening Europe (the Franco-German corps, for example). In 1991, it was almost uncanny how joint German-
U.S. announcements one week were followed by Franco-
German statements the next. There was particular irony
in the fact that the nation arbitrating between France and
the United States did not share many of their common
values concerning international security and could not participate in the kinds of out-of-area operations they envis-
aged. What is striking is how little effort was made by the
French and Americans to achieve common ground.

Establishing a New Partnership with France

Under the Clinton presidency and Balladur premiership, the clash of French and U.S. theses on European security has moved closer to coexistence or even synthesis. The Clinton administration has already reestablished communication that, under the Baker leadership, had virtually ended below the presidential level. It has been less apt to look for "special relationships" with individual European nations, which in practice meant Germany or Britain to the detriment of France, and has taken an open mind toward the concept of ESDI. At the same time, despite some resistance from the Elysée, Balladur and Juppé have acted forcefully to improve relations with the United States.

Although the events of the last two years have seriously undermined the credibility of the Maastricht Treaty, the French will want to do nothing that vitiates remaining prospects for European security cooperation or that weakens the possibility of creating a European Community with sufficient coherence to develop a common security and defense policy in the long term. The French will try to preserve as much as possible of their vision of a European Community qua superpower, as a France writ large, even if they recognize that they are now fighting an uphill battle.

At the same time, the French discovered that the only way of making ESDI real and operational was to secure NATO (and thus U.S.) support for it; that it is difficult to resolve even purely European issues like Bosnia without U.S. involvement (in this case, France had to push the United States to become *more* involved); and finally that potential threats from Russia require a U.S. military presence in Europe as well as NATO's survival. Under these circumstances, not surprisingly there has been an increasing amount of practical cooperation between the two countries. What is surprising is the extent of agreement on theological issues achieved at the NATO summit.

The U.S.-French relationship will be above all a security relationship. That seems a paradox, given the long record of conflict between the United States and France over NATO. That conflict, however, demonstrates a basic point: that both the United States and France define security policy as a fundamental national interest, that both conceive of national defense in global terms and maintain militaries capable of intervention all over the globe (naturally, on a different scale).

The period immediately following the end of the cold war brought much speculation that the post–cold war world would be dominated by economics, not military power. It was fashionable to view the United States and France as the big losers of that transformation and Germany and Japan as the big winners. Today, it is more commonly believed that even if the end of the cold war reduced the prospect for large-scale nuclear Armageddon, the amount of political and military conflict in the world has not diminished.

At a time when the United States wishes to concentrate on a domestic agenda (which also involves increasing its international economic competitiveness), it cannot escape a major international political and security role without running the risk of serious global instability. Thus, the United States needs allies who also define their interests as global and who are willing to act globally. Of our European allies, only the French and to a lesser extent the British fit this definition today. France alone may be able to mobilize the EU states behind this kind of global engagement.

In the long term, a tough and independent Europe, willing and able to play an international role, would be a welcome ally of a United States that needs to devote more of its resources to domestic concerns and wants to share its global burdens. Such a Europe would certainly be preferable to one that, without EU leadership, has returned to the internecine conflicts of the past or one that defines itself, under German influence, as a purely regional power. The complexity of dealing with a Europe capable of being a global partner, on the French model, may irritate us in the short term, but in the long run U.S.-European interests will converge along a range of issues from nonproliferation to environmentally sound economic growth in the Third World. The United States shares with France an appreciation that, given the world is still a dangerous place, a role exists for the prudent exercise of power and military force.

At the same time, no amount of common interest on security will eliminate differences over specific security issues (the devil is often in the details) or quarrels over other issues, particularly economics. Tensions over economic competition and trade, often based on disagreements about the appropriate role of the state in economic life, could become as divisive in the future as differences over security were in the past, unless kept in perspective. Because of the widespread negative attitudes that persist among both the elites and the general publics of both countries concerning the other, special care must be taken to avoid escalating disagreements into disputes that can genuinely prejudice the relationship. Indeed, only if Franco-U.S. relations become a priority for leaders at the highest level of each country are they likely to survive the legacy of accumulated bad will and mistrust.

Conclusion

Does France still count? What kind of role will post-cold war France play in Europe and the world? Does France have the domestic political cohesion and will to support its desire for European and international influence? Certainly, the great majority of the political class does have the cohesion and will to maintain French international influence and has been generally successful in doing so in recent decades. Perhaps no European country has been so effective in translating its potential into political influence.

The French public has not been consulted on most questions of high politics and has generally been willing to defer to its leaders. That deference may no longer be automatic, however. The referendum on Maastricht dramatically demonstrated the gulf between the elites and masses. One may argue that the elites will learn the lesson. Never again will a referendum of this sort be tried. On the other hand, a new generation of politicians like Philippe Séguin is trying to make its career by playing on popular misgivings about Europe. This tactic could lead to the breakdown of the consensus of the political class that has crystallized in the last decade, jeopardizing the continuity and stability of French policy toward Europe and the world.

To forestall such demagoguery, the political elite must address the sources of public discontent—first of all, the economy. The motor of French malaise has been unemployment. But there's the rub. For almost two decades, Europe has failed to resolve this problem, although it has been able to palliate it with social service programs. But the sluggish economy brings into question the possibility of maintaining such programs on their present scale. Full employment is the basis of social peace, and in the end social peace is the precondition for all else. But can full employment be attained? Can it be attained by national governments? By the EU? Although national electorates choose governments, the governments they choose become less and less able to affect the economic health of their nations.

Second, unless the political system is more responsive to the citizen, there is always the threat of a dangerous gap between the elite and the people. Further decentralizing power as well as finding ways to make Parliament a more vibrant institution would help narrow the gap. The way to stop demagoguery is to educate the public and involve the public. Third, it is hard to imagine the political system will respond to the citizen without a radical change in party structure. The replacement of old parties, which reflect yesterday's issues, by parties that reflect the concerns of today would make it easier to channel public concerns and educate the general public. The declining support for traditional parties in the legislative elections of 1993 and European elections of June 1994 sounds a warning. Although change would be disruptive in the short term, its alternative might be a dysfunctional political system.

Those who deplore the excessive populism of U.S. politics can only admire the way the French political elite has intelligently led the nation over recent decades. But more and more one finds oneself echoing Napoleon's mother, *"pourvu que ça dure...."* Despite these considerations, probably no country in Europe has a political system and political class better equipped to continue to exert political leadership than France. But political leadership where and how?

One of the major accomplishments of the rethinking of French policy after the cold war and the unification of Germany was the implicit recognition that French political leadership no longer meant leadership as an independent nation-state but as part of Europe – a recognition that France had to trade sovereignty for influence. For a country that prided itself so much on its independence, this is a major policy shift. France cannot be a political leader except within Europe. But the habits of the past survive even conscious political choices. France has a long tradition of acting in an adversarial relationship as a *franc tireur* and has not hesitated to block policies it does not like by "empty seat" tactics or by vetoes. But France cannot be both a leader in the EC and a blocking minority. Just as Germany cannot be the economic leader of Europe if it allows its Bundesbank to act against the interests of the European Union broadly defined, so France cannot be Europe's political leader if it is a roadblock to, rather than a shaper of, consensus.

France cannot be a political leader in Europe without continuing the Franco-German relationship. Indeed, without that relationship, there cannot be a stable Europe. Whatever problems have emerged since 1992, there is no choice but for France and Germany to forge ahead, to learn the lessons of their mistakes, to readjust strategy and tactics. Germany needs France as well, because Germany can never run Europe alone – and knows it.

Finally, French leadership in Europe cannot continue unless there is a serious and sustained rapprochement between France and the United States. Good relations between Europe and the United States are more important than ever before precisely because the collapse of the USSR has undermined the common threat that set strict parameters on internecine conflicts. France could afford to play itself off against the United States at a time when the

West was condemned to stand together in case of crisis. Political miscalculations today, however, can seriously damage Western solidarity at a time when new threats are already on the horizon but not clearly defined. France's atavistic propensity to try to score debating points against the United States or NATO does not contribute to Western solidarity, although it often is a reaction to Washington's obliviousness to French sensitivities. Yet that solidarity remains essential to prevent any possible recurrence of national conflicts in Western Europe and constitutes the major peace interest in the world today.

If France cannot provide political leadership in Europe today, there probably will be no leadership, only drift. If the United States cannot supply leadership in the West, there will be no leadership, only drift. Serious U.S.-French cooperation began in 1994. It must be nurtured and developed.

Notes

Chapter 1

1. For a concise history of the Franco-German relationship, see Julius W. Friend, *The Linchpin: French-German Relations, 1950–1990* (Washington, D.C.: Center for Strategic and International Studies/Praeger, 1991). A brief essay on the subject is Steven Philip Kramer, "France and the New Germany," in *German Issues* 11 (Washington, D.C.: American Institute for Contemporary German Studies, 1993). Also see Raymond Poidevin and Jacques Bariéty, *Les Relations franco-allemandes, 1815–1975* (Paris: Armand Colin, 1977). For the postwar period, F. Roy Willis, *France, Germany and the New Europe, 1945–1967*, rev. ed. (Stanford: Stanford University Press, 1968) is indispensable. A follow-up is provided by Haig Simonian, *The Privileged Partnership: Franco-German Relations in the European Community, 1969–1984* (Oxford: Oxford University Press, 1985). Alfred Grosser, *Affaires extérieures, la politique de la France, 1944–1989* (Paris: Flammarion, 1989) provides a good survey of French foreign policy. Jean Monnet, *Memoirs* (Garden City, N.Y.: Doubleday, 1978) gives an inside view of the creation of Europe.

2. France is the second largest economy and second largest trading nation in Western Europe and the fourth largest economy in the Western industrialized world. Its 1991 gross domestic product was estimated at $1,080 billion as compared with the Federal Republic of Germany's $1,398 billion and the United

Kingdom's $920.6 billion. *The World Fact Book 1993* (Langley, Va.: Central Intelligence Agency).

3. "Die Mark und die Bombe," *Die Zeit,* December 9, 1988.

4. On Mitterrand's foreign policy, Julius W. Friend, *Seven Years in France: François Mitterrand and the Unintended Revolution 1981–1988* (Boulder, Colo.: Westview, 1989), 195–213. For a more detailed narrative, see Pierre Favier and Michel-Martin Roland, *La Décennie Mitterrand* (Paris: Seuil, 1990).

5. François Cornut-Gentille and Stéphane Rozès, "La Réunification vue de l'Hexagone: les Français engourdis," in *L'Etat de l'opinion 1991* (Paris: Seuil, 1991), 75–91.

6. The most significant contribution to declinist thinking was Paul Kennedy, *The Rise and Fall of Great Powers* (New York: Random House, 1987).

7. Willis, *France, Germany and the New Europe,* 292–299.

8. From *Bulletin d'Information,* distributed by the French government to its embassies.

9. On the Bundesbank, see Ellen Kennedy, *The Bundesbank: Germany's Central Bank in the International Monetary System* (London: Chatham House, 1991), and David Marsh, *The Bundesbank: The Bank That Rules Europe* (London: Heinemann, 1992).

10. Ole Waever, "Three Competing Europes: German, French, Russian," *International Affairs* 66, no. 3 (July 1990): 484.

11. "'Vom Gemeinsamen Haus Europ' zur 'Europäischen Konföderation'—François Mitterrand und die europäische Neuordnung 1986–1990," *Sozialwissenschaftliche Informationen,* Heft 4/90.

12. George Lichtheim, *The New Europe* (New York: Praeger, 1965), 274.

Chapter 2

1. French security can best be understood in the context of French history as a whole. A good general French history text is Gordon Wright, *France in Modern Times,* 4th ed. (New York: Norton, 1981).

2. On Indochina, Algeria, and Suez, see Grosser, *Affaires extérieures.*

3. On the general lines of French interwar policy, Arnold Wolfers, *Britain and France between Two Wars* (New York: Harcourt, Brace, 1940). See also Poidevin and Bariéty, *Les Relations*

franco-allemandes; Philippe Bernard and Henry Dubief, *The Decline of the Third Republic, 1914–1938* (Cambridge: Cambridge University Press, 1985). The defeatist flavor of the 1930s is captured in Alexander Werth, *The Twilight of France, 1933–1940* (New York: Harper, 1942), and Denis W. Brogan, *France under the Republic, 1870–1939* (New York: Harper, 1940).

4. On the EDC, see Willis, *France, Germany and the New Europe*, 130–184, and Georgette Elgey, *La République des Tourments, 1954–1959* (Paris: Fayard, 1992), 165–259.

5. De Gaulle can best be approached through his own words, particularly through *The Complete War Memoirs*, 3 vols. (New York: Simon and Schuster, 1964). A full account of his life is Jean Lacouture, *De Gaulle*, 3 vols. (Paris: Seuil, 1984–1986). His enmity toward the United States can be traced to the wartime experience: Arthur Layton Funk, *Charles de Gaulle: The Crucial Years, 1943–1944* (Norman: University of Oklahoma Press, 1959).

6. For the impact of de Gaulle on his successors, see Philip H. Gordon, *A Certain Idea of France: French Security Policy and the Gaullist Legacy* (Princeton: Princeton University Press, 1993). On France's relationship to NATO after leaving the integrated military command, see Frédéric Bozo, *La France et l'OTAN: de la guerre froide au nouvel ordre européen* (Paris: Masson, 1991).

7. *Le Monde*, December 9–10, 1990.

8. *Le Monde*, February 6, 1991, and *France Statements* (French Embassy Press and Information Service), March 4, 1991.

Chapter 3

1. Each country's currency has a central exchange rate linked to the ECU (European Currency Unit). This is used to determine central rates for each pair of currencies. Bilateral exchange rates are allowed to fluctuate within a band around the central rate.

2. *International Herald Tribune*, January 27, 1994.

Chapter 4

1. For de Gaulle's perceptions of the problems of the French political system, see his memoirs. For the breakdown of the

Third Republic, Bernard and Dubief, *Decline of the Third Republic*; Jean-Pierre Azéma, *From Munich to the Liberation, 1938–1944* (Cambridge: Cambridge University Press, 1985), which also deals with the occupation and resistance. On Vichy in particular, see Robert Paxton, *Vichy France: Old Guard and New Order, 1940–1944* (New York: Knopf, 1972). In *France under the Republic*, Brogan gives an unparalleled account of how the Third Republic worked. Two classics are David Thomson, *Democracy in France since 1870*, 5th ed. (Oxford: Oxford University Press, 1969), and Stanley Hoffmann, *In Search of France* (Cambridge: Harvard University Press, 1963). Gordon Wright, *The Reshaping of French Democracy* (New York: Reynal and Hitchcock, 1948) explains why de Gaulle failed to change French political institutions after the war. See also, Steven Philip Kramer, "The Provisional Republic: The Collapse of the French Resistance Front and the Origins of Post-War Politics 1944–1946," Ph.D. diss., Princeton University, 1971. On the Fourth Republic, Jean-Pierre Rioux, *The Fourth Republic, 1944–1958* (Cambridge: Cambridge University Press, 1987). The best account of how the Fifth Republic functions is Vincent Wright, *The Government and Politics of France*, 3rd ed. (New York: Holmes and Meier, 1989).

2. On the coup, see Maurice Agulhon, *The Republican Experiment, 1848–1852* (Cambridge: Cambridge University Press, 1983).

3. On May 1968, see Bernard E. Brown, *Protest in Paris: Anatomy of a Revolt* (Morristown, N.J.: General Learning Press, 1974).

4. For an introduction to the vast literature on the Popular Front, see Bernard and Dubief, *Decline of the Third Republic*.

5. On Mitterrand and the PS, see Friend, *Seven Years*.

6. For background on the PCF, see Jacques Fauvet, *Histoire du parti communiste français de 1920 à 1976*, 2nd ed. (Paris: Fayard, 1977).

7. Gérard Le Gall, "L'Effet immigration," in *L'Etat de l'opinion 1991*, 119–136.

8. Brogan gives detailed treatment to Third Republic scandals. See also Philip Williams, *Wars, Plots and Scandals in Post-War France* (Cambridge: Cambridge University Press, 1970).

9. To place the Front National within the French political tradition, see René Rémond, *Les Droites en France*, 4th ed. (Paris: Aubier-Montaigne, 1982). On the FN, see Edwy Plenel and Alain Rollat, *L'Effet Le Pen* (Paris: La Decouverte, 1984).

10. Olivier Duhamel and Gérard Grunberg, "Référendum: les dix France," *L'Etat de l'opinion 1993*, 79–86.

Chapter 5

1. Christoph Bertram, "Visions of Leadership: Germany," in Steven Muller and Gebhard Schweigler, *From Occupation to Cooperation: The United States and United Germany in a Changing World Order* (New York: Norton, 1992), 66.

2. For two recent contributions to the debate on U.S.-French security dialogue, see Pierre Lellouche, "France in Search of Security," *Foreign Affairs* 72, no. 2 (Spring 1993), and Robert P. Grant, *The Changing Franco-American Security Relationship* (Arlington, Va.: U.S. Crest, 1993).

Index

ISBN 0-275-95060-3

90000>

EAN

9 780275 950606

HARDCOVER BAR CODE